SURVIVE AND THRIVE THROUGH YOUR SEPARATION

AN EASY GUIDE TO LEGAL, PRACTICAL AND EMOTIONAL ASPECTS OF SEPARATION AND DIVORCE IN AUSTRALIA

HELEN SLATER

The material in this book is provided for information purposes only.

www.HelenSlater.com.au

helen@helenslater.com.au

© Helen Slater 2020

The moral rights of the author have been asserted.

All rights reserved. This book may not be reproduced in whole or in part, stored, posted on the internet, or transmitted in any form or by any means, electronic, mechanical, photocopying, recording, or other, without written permission from the author of the book.

Cover Design: Lana Pecherczyk

ISBN: 978-0-6450515-0-6 (Ebook)

ISBN: 978-0-6450515-1-3 (Paperback)

*For my children, I love you, I love you, I love you,
and my parents Eric and Carol Slater,
I love you, and Thank You!*

DISCLAIMER

This book covers some legal information pertaining to Australian family law. This book should not be taken or substituted for legal advice. Although I ultimately represented myself in court, I am not a qualified or practicing lawyer. The information in this book is intended to provide people who are going through a separation, or similar proceedings, with an overview of what they may encounter in the process and should not be taken as legal advice. It is important you seek independent legal advice specific to your situation.

As the author, I assume no responsibility for liability, loss or risk, financial, personal or otherwise, that is incurred as a consequence, whether directly or indirectly, in regards to any of the contents in this book.

For confidentiality reasons some details have been changed to protect privacy.

On a final note, although a little humour and light-hearted banter has been used in this book (to help maintain your sanity!), I by no means intend to trivialise your circumstances or make light of the intensity of your situation, I can empathise as I've been there and it is truly a challenging time.

CONTENTS

Acknowledgements	9
Foreword	13
Written By Lucy Good, founder of Beanstalk Mums	
Introduction	17
Chapter 1	27
SEPARATING FROM YOUR PARTNER	
Chapter 2	58
PROPERTY AND MONEY	
Chapter 3	85
CHILDREN AND PARENTING	
Chapter 4	112
LEGAL PROCESS AND COURT PROCEEDINGS	
Chapter 5	153
LAWYERS, LEGAL ADVICE, LEGAL COSTS and LEGAL WORDS	
Chapter 6	187
MY STORY	
Helpful Websites and Resources	201
Bibliography	203
Notes	207
About the Author	213

ACKNOWLEDGEMENTS

To my children, thank you for your endless supply of hugs and kisses and words of encouragement. I love you, I love you, I love you!

To my parents, who after over fifty years of marriage continue to laugh and enjoy life to the fullest, thank you for always being there for me from across the miles, love you both.

My soul sister, Delia Wright, thank you for always encouraging me to share my light.

Graham Hughes, my friend and mentor for over twenty-five years, whose advice, love and attention keeps me inspired and accountable. Thank you.

Thank you and gratitude to my friends and family, in particular:

Wendy O, for being with me every step of the way, for her faith in my abilities and wanting to be first in line to buy my book.

Sue H, for opening her home to me and my girls when we needed it most.

Tiffany G, always there with a listening ear and a quick-witted reply.

Stacey, my walking buddy, sounding board and second mum to Rolo.

Debbie, my own personal, butt-kicking, accountability friend who's watched this book come to be over the past ten years.

Sue M, always on hand to help with childminding, sleepovers and school runs.

Larissa, my good friend and coffee connoisseur!

Mike, our 'adopted' Grandad and on-call handyman.

Tom, for being the first positive Aussie male role model for my girls, and for our one on one lunches with red wine and laughter.

Erin, Avril and Amanda, part of my 'Saturday Night' girls posse.

John W, who without knowing it helped start me on my journey through 'Inner Learning'.

Alexandra K, whose eye for detail and expert feedback meant I was able to sleep peacefully at night.

Pippa C for her savvy legal advice and Amanda L for her legal hand-holding all those years ago.

Lucy Good, founder of *Beanstalk Mums* and a fellow kindred spirit, thank you for your kind words and agreeing to write the foreword.

To my clients who trust me to be a part of their life.

And you, the reader, I hope that this book helps you on your own journey of separation.

FOREWORD

WRITTEN BY LUCY GOOD, FOUNDER OF BEANSTALK MUMS

My separation was a blur! I distinctly remember the realisation that I had become (dramatic pause) a single mum. It was a few weeks after I actually became one, which gives you an idea of the state of my life at the time.

Amid the blur, I remember my main thought. It was simple: 'Where can I find help?'. I was right at the start of my single mother journey. I needed support now and knew I was going to need it later. Show me one single mum who doesn't ask themselves this question when they first separate and I'll YouTube myself dancing in my undies. It's a scary, unknown time which impacts us on every level and in every area of our lives.

There were two things I desperately wanted in my search for help: guidance for the practical side of my separation in the form of clear, understandable advice, and to feel less alone.

Helen, where were you back then when I needed you?

This book is gold dust for anyone going through a separation, and in particular a newly single mum. I'll say it again … GOLD DUST.

Helen has done the most empowering thing of all. She has taken a part of her life that was a pretty rough ride (sorry if that is a huge understatement Helen) and has shared her learnings, her mistakes, her insights and her own personal experience to help others.

No one tells it like Helen does! With the answers you need to navigate the family court either alone or along-side your lawyer, each page is a treasure trove of invaluable information to lower your stress levels, save you money and give you the courage to keep going.

Helen and I are kindred spirits. Through our work and our passion to give single mums a clear path and quick access to their wonderful new lives (yes, your life will too be wonderful), we have become friends. Helen is a clever, fun, capable, strong women. When you read this book, she will become your friend and a key part of your support circle.

I work with hundreds of single mums every day, I have my own story and know so many others. The most important piece of advice I give these ladies is to educate themselves. This no longer means hunting down information from various (possibly dubious) resources. It is all here in this book.

I would have given my right arm to have had a resource like this when I first separated and became a single mum. You are so lucky you get to embark on the most valuable learning experience of your separation with all your original body parts intact.

Enjoy!

INTRODUCTION

The first thing you should know is that I am not a lawyer, I did however represent myself in legal proceedings.

It all started whilst I was going through the process of separation and trying to agree on children's arrangements, property settlement and divorce. I was frustrated at the lack of succinct and easy-to-understand information that could help explain the legal process, the structure, the paperwork and documents, the people who would be involved and the associated costs; and that's why this book came to be.

With no legal training or prior legal knowledge whatsoever, I survived family law legal proceedings predominantly as a self-represented litigant, and my hope is that by sharing my legal journey with you and the insights I gained along the way, as well as introducing you to some coaching frameworks, you'll be better able to take control of your separation and your life in general.

Within these pages I recount my journey and describe:

- what happened
- what I found out and the options that were available
- how I did it
- who was involved
- what I did and why
- the ultimate outcomes of my choices

I'll also include some clarity about legal jargon and aspects of the formal separation process.

Going through the journey of a separation and/or legal proceedings is challenging and stressful:

- emotionally (feelings)
- physically (body)
- mentally (thoughts)
- spiritually (beliefs)
- financially (money)
- socially (family/friends)

The aim of sharing my experience with you is to help lower your stress levels by providing some knowledge, insight and empathy along with helpful tips, techniques and strategies to embrace change, feel empowered, get organised and ultimately help 'save your sanity and your savings'!

By the end of this book, you will have a greater understanding of some aspects of the legal process of Australian family law, specifically in relation to separation. Written in straightforward language, it covers:

- the process: a big picture overview
- the stages and structure: timings and outcomes
- the paperwork: the documents involved
- the roles and responsibilities: the people involved and what they do, and your role too
- the associated costs: legal fees, court fees and other expenses
- the potential outcomes: offers, agreements, Orders and settlements
- the language of law: the jargon

This is my story. It's by no means the 'norm' or the right way or wrong way, the hard way, the usual way or the easy way. It was just my way.

Naively, I was of the belief that when I separated I would have to go to court to sort out the money, the property and children's arrangements and use the services of a lawyer to speak to a Judge, when actually that's not necessarily the case.

Many people benefit from counselling or mediation, however, in my case that was not to be, and I ended up in the legal system attending court many times during my legal proceedings.

Initially, I had had the legal support of a local law firm, who were incredibly understanding of my situation; though due to the nature of my matter and the frustration of my ex-husband's behaviour, self-representing seemed the most sensible (yet terrifying) option. So, after some initial hand-holding and to save what little money I had, I decided to self-represent and threw myself into the process.

To say that legal proceedings were not an easy journey is an understatement. Fraught with sleepless nights, I often lay awake wondering how it would impact the children, where the children would live and with whom, where I would live, and how I would explain it all to them. Then I'd worry about the finances: where the money would come from, whether there was any money at all, who had it, who would get it, how much legal fees would cost, and on and on it went.

I recall many nights compiling data, collating evidence, completing documents and drafting affidavits until two in the morning. On a few occasions the presiding Judge made reference to my material and quoted the timeframe with raised eyebrows and a smile (*'I refer to the Applicant mother's email of 19 July at 02.11am'*)!

Interestingly, during my separation my divorce was the easiest (turned out to be more of a paper exercise); property settlement was the most frustrating and children's custody and arrangements the most challenging.

Often people incorrectly refer to a divorce in the context of property settlement and custody of children when in fact a divorce is purely a paper exercise, an application to legally end your relationship.

There's a lot of information out there on separation and the legal process; having to wade through it all could take you hours, weeks, months even years to gain an insight into what you're wanting an answer for, after all, lawyers study for years to be able to understand it, share the knowledge and keep your best interests at heart.

Needless to say, this is not a comprehensive guide to family law, it's more of a quick overview of what you may come across during your dealings and interactions within the legal process, from paperwork to people.

I think it's fair to say that many people are unaware of the information and services available to them outside the realms of a lawyer's office or courtroom; whether that be mediation, arbitration or collaborative law (more on these later). Oh, and by the way, the word 'fair' is not used in court – it's too subjective; 'fair' is replaced with 'just and equitable'.

As we are all unique, so too are our situations. No experience is ever the same. We all have our own set of circumstances and expectations, and they will ultimately impact our outcomes. However, that said, there is commonality in areas of the process, for example, the initial documents and information, statutory deadlines and likely timeframes, expectations, roles and responsibilities.

Separation is an emotional time and even though everyone's situation and circumstances are different, the stress and challenges impact most of us in similar ways.

Let's begin with how you came to be reading this book.

I'm going to assume that you (or someone you know) are going through a separation and are seeking legal information to understand what happens next or at least what to expect. Perhaps you haven't quite left the relationship physically, though you have left it emotionally and are now proactively getting your facts together and preparing your next move. Or perhaps you've already separated and need closure on the situation. Perhaps your former partner has initiated proceedings and you're now in 'reactionary' mode.

Whether a friend has recommended this book to you, or you've borrowed or bought it, you're about to have a quick education, an overview if you like, on aspects of the process of family law in Australia and strategies to survive and thrive through this challenging time in your life.

To reiterate, my aim for this book is to help you:

- navigate your way through a separation
- gain a simple overview of legal proceedings
- understand the roles of those involved

- save on legal fees
- understand some legal jargon
- feel empowered within the process
- provide you with some coping strategies

I've been involved in personal development my whole working life, and I continue to use and develop strategies and frameworks to help progress positively in both my mentoring and coaching business, (6S Coaching – say it aloud and it makes sense), as well as in my personal life, whether that's in the context of relationships, goals, direction, behaviour, finances, creativity, parenting, you name it and I'll have a strategy for it, and if not, I'll develop one!

Throughout this book you'll be introduced to some strategies and frameworks to support you through your separation, or any life challenge, to enable you to come out the other side stronger. I'll make reference to my 6S six-step strategies, strategies that have worked for me not only during my separation, but for over thirty years in all aspects of my life.

Let me introduce one now. I first encountered a variation of this six-step strategy in 1992 when I joined a successful management consultant to progress and evolve his business. Our main goals were around change management, and with that in mind, we conducted research into which organisations had the most success with habit changing; the result...drug rehabilitation centres and Alcoholics Anonymous. A funny story, when we first started asking questions of AA on their twelve-step process for change, they actually thought we were alcoholics who were in denial. I must admit, I do like a glass of red wine, but not to the extent where I'd need to seek support (though if I did need help, it's likely this would be the organisation I'd go to!). From our research, we developed a simple six-step strategy and introduced it to our existing and potential clients; the results spoke for themselves, and the fact that I continue to use it today, over twenty-five years later, is a testament to its success.

Over the years I adapted it further and here it is in its current 6S format:

1. START [acceptance] – accept the need for change. Acknowledge your starting point; when you know your starting point, you can move and progress from there. Be proactive.
2. SHARE [awareness] – be aware of both your external situation and your internal mindset. Share your thinking, feelings and situation with another. Identify areas that need attention.
3. SIMPLIFY [support] – get back to basics, declutter your 'space' (your headspace as well as your physical space). Gain a support team to help in all areas: emotional, mental, physical, spiritual, social, legal and practical.
4. STRATEGY [hold on, let go] – clarify your big picture, your starting point, your in-between points, and your end point. Look at strengths and weaknesses of the situation and yourself; focus on your strengths, let go of your weaknesses.

5. STRUCTURE [create new ways] – create your Action Plan: the what, why, where, when, who and how to make it happen.
6. SUSTAIN [sustain the change] – evaluate your progress, celebrate your successes and sustain success with effective habits and accountability.

Now, it's fair to say that those who know me best know that I like to do things a little differently and I want to get you thinking and feeling differently too, so that you can embrace change. Ever heard of the quote, 'If you always do what you've always done, you'll always get what you've always got'?

For now, having an idea of the big picture and knowing what we'll be talking about means we can take one step at a time, not be overwhelmed, be able to identify thoughts, feelings and behaviours, as well as identify relevant information and from there clarify manageable bite size actions.

I'd like to think that you can read this book in its entirety in a short time frame, perhaps a few early mornings over coffee or in the evening (with a glass of wine?). Read and re-read. Use it as a reference guide too. Get the overview information and 'take stock' of your thoughts (aka your mindset, more on mindset a little later).

I'm sure if you'd ask any lawyer, they'd agree that someone having a little knowledge on a big scale is more harmful than helpful. Asking relevant questions and providing the most appropriate answers is a two-way street between both you and your lawyer. Do not be afraid to ask, to speak up, to seek clarity, to gain advice and to express your concerns and ideals. Engage in the process fully, whether that's with you or your lawyer taking the reins.

My intention is to shed some light on the potentially challenging journey of separation and to share the basics with you so that you:

- have a heads-up on aspects of the process
- are equipped to ask relevant questions
- have an idea of expectations
- are introduced to some coping strategies and some of my 6S coaching frameworks that will complement your situation, including your relationship with yourself, your ex, and your lawyer

I'm excited to be sharing my knowledge and experience with you! I hope you gain some insights and feel empowered to embrace this new chapter of your life.

Let's begin.

1

SEPARATING FROM YOUR PARTNER

It's Over! Separating from your partner is more manageable when you have a positive mindset. Easier said than done, right?!

So, you've decided it's over, or your partner has. What now?

My ex made the decision it was over. The long and short of it is that my husband left, and I was alone and isolated on a rental acreage with two young children, a large dog, no job, hardly any money in the bank and no family or friends around me for support.

We attended counselling to address some of our issues, unfortunately there was no happy ending and legal proceedings commenced six months later.

With statistics showing that around two in three marriages in Australia ends in divorce,[1] it's not unreasonable to assume that everyone knows someone who is considering separating, has already separated or is in the thick of it.

Typically, family law matters are addressed as three main aspects:

- Children Arrangements
- Property Settlement
- Divorce

Just as a point of clarity, I'd like to mention that there's a difference between 'legal proceedings' and courtroom attendance, and that you don't necessarily need to be in a courtroom to be involved in legal proceedings.

Depending on how amicable you are with your ex, you can resolve things together, with or without lawyers. In fact, you may not need a lawyer at all, maybe just a good counsellor.[2] Sometimes just hearing what your partner has to say, and for them to hear what you have to say, can be enough to start the process of getting your relationship back on track or at least to separate on amicable terms.

Communication is key to:

- understanding perspectives
- resolving any issues

Perhaps this is a good time to briefly outline the definitions I use to differentiate between a counsellor, a therapist, a coach and a mentor. So, in very simplistic terms:

Counsellor – gives guidance on coping with personal challenges mentally or emotionally, and may address a specific issue like life transitions, better relationships, stress and anxiety. They can help provide clarity and strategies to assist in resolving problems.

Therapist – predominately concerned with addressing psychological issues. They often discuss the past to get to the root cause of a problem. It can be a long-term process.

Coach – typically helps clients identify what their ideal life looks like, helps set goals and create an action plan for attaining them. Coaching is solution focused and looks to the future; a coach helps motivate, inspire and empower others.

Mentor – has experience in what the client is going through and is able to provide guidance, knowledge and motivation, including emotional and practical support. Like a coach, a mentor helps motivate, inspire and empower others.

Whether I am supporting clients, meeting with lawyers, dealing with court representatives or interacting with friends and family, I am constantly mindful of how they communicate, how they react, the words they use, what's important to them and the outcomes they are wanting. This is where having some insight into their 'behavioural style' can assist in getting the best from them and the situation.

Let's explore 'behavioural styles' a little more. For this purpose I am using four main behavioural styles, namely:

- amiable
- analytical
- driver
- expressive

We usually display two main dominant styles, for example, you may discover you are an analytical driver, an amiable expressive, or a driving analyst, in fact we frequently move between the four styles. However, under pressure we will revert to our predominant style.

Now before you start comparing yourself to others, know that no one style is better than the other.

In very simple terms, here's my quick overview of each in a table diagram format:

Behavioural Style	Amiable	Analytical	Driver	Expressive
Main point of interest	PEOPLE orientated	DATA orientated	TASK orientated	IDEAS orientated
Traits and qualities	Supportive Reliable Friendly Diplomatic Cooperative Good listeners	Facts Accuracy Orderly Structured Persistent Organised	Direct Independent Takes risks Productive Authority Loves challenges	Lively Optimistic Enthusiastic Intuitive Persuasive Creative
Main focus and Strength	Collaboration	Planning	Goals Results	Vision Big Picture Ideas
Weakness	Submissive	Indecisive	Competitive	Impulsive
Key word	'We'	'Why'	'When'	

Identifying people's behavioural styles can improve the productivity and efficiency of your communication with them by giving you an insight into where and how to focus your attention. When you know what resonates with them you can affect thoughts, feelings, behaviour, focus, communication and all interactions.

For example, when communicating with an 'analyst' the best place to focus your energy would be in finding data or facts that best resonate with your argument or main point of view. Providing data to an 'expressive' would have the opposite effect; instead, providing them with the big picture and being open with your feelings would gain better results.

Having an awareness of how each of us behaves provides a good heads-up on how best to interact so that there's a higher likelihood of a win-win scenario.

Another point of reference is Love Languages.

Perhaps you've heard of the five love languages by Gary Chapman? The idea is that each of us feel and give love in certain ways. In summary, the five love languages are:

- acts of service
- gifts
- physical touch
- quality time
- words of appreciation[3]

If you can determine your predominate love language, and that of your partner, you may be in a better position to understand each other's perspective. For more information on the 5 Love Languages see www.5lovelanguages.com where you can also complete an online quiz to find out your personal love language(s).

Whether you decide to work on your relationship or work outside of the relationship, therapy, counselling and coaching is worth considering. It's likely that you'll explore the polarity of 'stay or go' and there'll likely be two main outcomes: 1) you'll decide on a strategy to progress with working on your relationship together, or 2) you'll decide the relationship is over and it's time to move on.

If you decide to separate and move on, it's always best to end in mutual agreement, with each of you accepting the end of the relationship. The 'blame game' will no doubt come into play, that's human nature, remember it's better to be out of an unhappy relationship than in one (I feel like I'm channelling Dr Phil!). That said, separating can be an expensive and emotionally challenging process and to help set expectations, I'd like to share my experience.

It took around six months for me to realise that my husband was not invested in our relationship and that he was not coming back; he continued to play the *I'm not sure, ask me again next month* card. After six months of checking-in with him, I reclaimed my independence, met with an accountant and a lawyer and started to proactively explore my options. I had a lightbulb moment: he was having his cake and eating it too. In the coming weeks I invited him to dinner and subsequently mediation. (There was no cake at either.)

If you were the one that was left by your partner, this can seem bewildering and shocking, particularly if it's without warning. Where possible, mutual agreement and an amicable separation is paramount to a smooth transition, particularly if there are children involved.

If an amicable separation is not to be (yes, they do exist) then consider the next phase as a 'project' and an opportunity to embrace the next chapter of your life. Have an open mind and grab it with both hands. Now *you* get to decide *your* goals, where *you* want to be, what *you* want to achieve and where to focus *your* energy. You'll have complete control and independence.

I believe there are two main motivators in life, the polarity of: the pursuit of pleasure and the avoidance of pain. To put it another way, our number one need is to be accepted and our number one fear is to be rejected.

It would be a reasonable assumption that at the start of your relationship you were in a pleasurable place, otherwise it's unlikely that you'd stay. Fast forward in time and now you're more than likely in the 'avoidance of pain' mode. Be proactive and take the reins, get organised, be present, be mindful, be objective and be strong. That way you can take control of the process, rather than letting the process take control of you.

An important point to note here: if you and your children are in harm's way you need to move quickly and safely.

If you or someone you know is in immediate danger, call '000'.

Domestic Violence is, sadly, widespread, with the following basic statistics showing the prevalence and severity of violence against women:[4]

- On average at least one woman is killed every nine days by a partner or former partner in Australia.
- One in six Australian women has experienced physical violence since the age of 15.
- One in five Australian women has experienced sexual violence.
- One in four Australian women has experienced physical or sexual violence by an intimate partner.

- One in four Australian women has experienced emotional abuse by a current or former partner.
- Women are at least three times more likely than men to experience violence from an intimate partner.
- Women are five times more likely than men to require medical attention or hospitalisation as a result of intimate partner violence, and five times more likely to report fearing for their lives.
- Of those women who experience violence, more than half have children in their care.

Let's address what Domestic Violence (DV) is and what it looks like, so that you can spot the signs and potential red flags, particularly as they can be very subtle[5].

Many people identify DV as physical harm, though it's more than broken bones and bruises, it's also about mental health and emotional wellbeing. I didn't even realise that DV was affecting me until after I had separated from my ex.

Let's look at some of the categories of abuse.

EMOTIONAL & PSYCHOLOGICAL ABUSE

There are many forms of emotional abuse: threats, emotional extortion and blackmail, threats of suicide, self-esteem erosion, constant criticising, undermining character, turning children against you, implying and spreading rumours of mental illness, invasion of privacy, 'Jekyll and Hyde' personality, mind games and gaslighting.[6] I define gaslighting as a form of psychological manipulation in which a person seeks to sow seeds of doubt in someone making them question their own memory, perception, and sanity.

My ex blamed me for all the problems in our relationship and undermined my self-worth and self-esteem with belittling statements. *'You've got issues', 'no wonder no one wants to be your friend', 'I can see why your relationships didn't last', 'you're ____ ____ ____ ____!'* I'll let you fill in the blanks.

Along with emotional abuse, there is usually verbal abuse.

VERBAL ABUSE

Name calling, whether it be to your face or electronically. Insults and putdowns, undercutting or interrupting you in conversations and subsequently dominating the conversation. Threats, lies, fault-finding, sarcasm and being indiscreet. Public humiliation, yelling and shouting, and conversely whispering, another is, ironically, giving you the silent treatment.[7]

Some of my DV experience was when I was in the relationship, though once the relationship was over, that's when my ex upped the ante. I was inundated with texts, emails, and voicemails, none of which were constructive.

What vexed me the most was that he also contacted my parents without my knowledge, and not in a good way. One particular email he sent directly to them was very disturbing and included an extensive list of lies. I was suffering from PSTD (I wasn't), I was severely depressed (I wasn't), I was going to harm myself and the children (I never would), I had affairs with the male neighbour (I hadn't), though conversely, he also called me a lesbian. The list was long and lengthy and upset my parents immensely. Fortunately, I have a great relationship with them and as a result they immediately forwarded the email to me. I reassured them that it was nonsense, but unfortunately the damage had already been done, my mum was in tears and my dad was left with is head in his hands, shaking his head in disbelief. Words really do hurt and cause harm, their impact goes deeper and lasts longer than physical pain.

FINANCIAL ABUSE

Taking complete control of the money and finances. Controlling the money in and the money out, everything from work-related income to welfare payments, to shopping expenditure and rationing or placing conditions on spending. Restricting account access, withdrawing joint funds without knowledge and permission, and concealing assets. Keeping financial affairs secrets. Running up debt. Other red flags are no job, refusing to work, disinterest in finding a job, taking monetary risks and gambling joint money.[8]

I shake my head when I reflect on this one, here's why: my ex had mentioned to me early in our relationship that as I was so independent he felt as though he didn't contribute much to the relationship. So in order to show him that we were on equal footing, I handed over the financial reins to him—big mistake, huge!

When I first met my ex I paid him rent to help towards his mortgage, again my values were and still are about independence and I wanted to be able to 'pay my own way' so to speak. Shortly after I sold my UK property (a house that had no mortgage attached to it as I had paid it off completely) and transferred the funds from my UK bank account to 'our joint' Australian bank account (which it turned out didn't need both signatures to access the funds), my ex subsequently transferred the majority of the funds into another account solely in his name without my knowledge.

When the time came for us to upgrade and buy a new place together, my ex found a house and arranged all the mortgage paperwork. He said he'd made an appointment with a mortgage broker and we were going to have a chat; turns out I was there to sign the mortgage documents! The dialogue went something like this:

'Sign here,' my ex said, pointing to the mortgage document.

'Do I get a chance to read it?'

'No need, just sign here.'

Because the mortgage broker was in the room, I assumed it was all above board and met our circumstances, even looking at the broker with my bewildered expression, he just said, 'It's all a go, [your husband] has confirmed it and provided all the necessary information.' It was only after signing and being sent the final documentation that I realised that my ex had 'fudged' some of the numbers, and we were going to be way over our heads in debt, particularly as he didn't have a job and I was now looking after a toddler, with our second child due in the following few weeks.

What really sticks out from the above is the coercion to sign legally binding documents (like mortgage documents, Wills and an Enduring Power of Attorney), and him not having a job. My ex still has challenges working, from making big bucks in construction when we first separated, to not making enough to pay child support. He's seldom paid child support in the past ten years and his child support debt is in the tens of thousands. It's worth noting that not paying child support is also a form of financial abuse.

My ex would send emails saying he has the money but he's not paying anything until I do *this* or do *that*, I explained that's not how it works. He then said if I didn't do what he wanted he would give the money away to a children's charity! Hmmm, Make A Wish foundation may be a few thousand dollars better off, yet our children were going without extracurricular activities as I couldn't afford them all. Swimming, music, sports and arts, something had to go.

What a non-paying child support parent fails to realise is that it's the children that miss out. To this day, my ex's child support assessment for the year would barely cover the cost of one child's school uniform and when I say one, I mean one; one top, one pair of shorts, one jacket, one hat, never mind school shoes, school resources, school excursions or any extracurricular activities. On the plus side, both of the children are keen to work and make their own money, and I'm teaching them about independence, specifically financial independence (a shout out here to Scott Pape aka the Barefoot Investor for sharing his easy to understand insights. If you haven't read Scott's books yet, do yourself a favour and get hold of a copy and make time to read them, you'll be glad you did!).

SOCIAL ABUSE

As the category suggests, social abuse relates to your interactions with others. The key factor here is isolation and restricting access to friends and family. Other factors are jealousy, accusations of affairs, controlling your appearance, needing your complete attention all the time, and sabotaging social engagements. Denigrating family and friends, controlling who you can and cannot see and speak to, monitoring your phone calls, text messages and emails, and even removing, throwing and/or smashing your mobile phone. Geographically isolating you from other people. Disallowing transport or having a driving licence and preventing social and/or employment opportunities.[9]

As all my family were in the UK, this was a particularly difficult time for me, both during my marriage and after. Even without the constraints of my ex's behaviour, talking with my friends and family in the UK was often challenging due to the distance and time difference.

When my marriage ended, naturally I wanted to visit my family, and my ex had originally agreed to this both before and during our counselling sessions. However, when it came to the reality of it, he wouldn't allow me and the children to go. He wouldn't sign the renewal forms for the children's passports, incidentally this then became another matter where I needed to seek the court's assistance.

Another aspect of social abuse is isolation. After our house sold, we decided to rent until we were ready to buy again. We looked at a couple of rental properties, one was close to where we had just sold, the other was in the middle of nowhere, 45 minutes away from the children's day care centre. Initially, the idea of moving away was to give our relationship a fresh start; we had agreed to get away from some of my ex's family dynamics and challenges, or so I thought. Turned out I was the one being isolated in the middle of nowhere, as my ex had agreed to rent a seafront unit close to his mother's home (without my knowledge) and was going to base himself there, he was leaving. All this he told me over the phone, on my birthday, at a time when I was surrounded by noisy toddlers as I collected the children from the day care centre. Memorable for sure!

STALKING & HARRASSMENT

I think everyone has an idea of stalking, the obvious is loitering around home, work, day care, school and public places like the local swimming pool, community library and turning up at or driving past any location that the other person frequents. Watching, following, or shadowing in public areas. Some other aspects are leaving unwanted messages and gifts.[10] Reading and taking mail (taking someone else's mail is a federal offence and can attract fines and even imprisonment[11]).

My ex stalked us at home, at the school, the local swimming pool, and the resort where my parents used to stay when they visited.

After months of being absent he reintroduced himself at approximately 7.30pm, standing under a dimly lit streetlamp, positioned at the exit ramp of the undercover car park of the resort my parents were staying, raising his hand slowly as we drove out. When I got home, he was already parked outside my house. While I got the sleeping toddlers out of the car, he creeped up the driveway and whispered in my ear. It was totally unnerving, and I told him to leave otherwise I'd call the police. He loitered around and eventually left after I went inside.

My ex's actions also consisted of relentless texts, emails, phone calls and disturbing voicemails. He not only harassed me but my elderly parents and extended family too, leaving voicemails or just hanging up, day and night. On a few occasions he called at midnight and continued calling half a dozen times through the night. My parents ended up having to block the number he was calling from.

I moved three times to get away from him. He would send emails saying he knew where I lived, or, 'I know you've sold your car.' I had! He always seemed to know where I lived, yet he refused to tell me where he lived; even during our court proceedings his address was listed as unknown and information pertaining to his address was listed as his mother's home address. To this day his residential address is still unknown to me.

Another form of stalking is when someone gets others involved. One evening when I was putting my bins out, I opened my front door and his brother's business card (who lives out of state) was strategically placed in the door frame. This got my heart racing, it was intimidating. For almost ten years I have had the same PO Box for receiving correspondence and parcels, yet around the same time that the brother's business card was left, I received two parcels from my ex at my home address. His message was yet again subtle: I know where you live. I immediately went out and bought a gate lock. That evening I decided enough was enough and made an appointment with a solicitor to seek legal advice. Clear correspondence was sent to my ex, nothing changed and subsequently an application for a protection order followed.

TECHNOLOGY

Tracking whereabouts via mobile, monitoring access via online banking, threats via social media, threats to share intimate photos, limiting internet access, getting others to monitor via social media, posting false information online.[12]

My ex posted lies on social media, for example, falsely accusing me of kidnapping the children.

SEXUAL

Sexual assault and/or harassment, or any unwanted or forced sexual act or behaviour without consent. Rationing or denial of sex; unwanted involvement in pornography, sharing intimate photos and videos; denying contraception, and forced abortion.[13]

CULTURAL/SPIRITUAL

Ridiculing beliefs, demanding you take on their beliefs, denying choices, and the misuse of cultural and religious beliefs to justify behaviours.[14]

PHYSICAL

Slapping, hitting, hair pulling, punching, choking, strangling, spitting, throwing objects, damage to possessions, reckless driving, use of weapons, being locked inside or outside. Harm to children. Cruelty to pets. Murder or attempted murder.[15] These are just some examples it is by no means a comprehensive list.

As physical harm is more obvious than some of the other categories of DV, here's a quick metaphor to help highlight the potential risk of being exposed to DV particularly when we are often too close to the situation to see the danger.

The Boiling Frog

Imagine a frog in a pan of warm water; at first the frog feels safe and warm, then the water is slowly heated. As the temperature heats up, the frog adjusts its body temperature to match the heating water, it does not perceive the danger of the situation. Eventually, at boiling point, the frog can't adapt anymore and decides to jump out but having lost all its strength due to constantly adjusting, it can't get out and subsequently perishes.

If we look at this from a DV perspective we can observe how at the start of a relationship it may feel nice, warm and cosy, the feeling of being taken care of, yet as things gradually start to 'heat up', usually with subtle manipulations, it's at this point that the boiling has started and you adapt, unaware of where it may be leading you. Then, at the point where you feel it's time to get out, you don't have the resources, energy or courage to get out alone.

It's important to see the gradual changes, decide to 'jump out' and take action whilst you still have the strength.

Remember though to keep a healthy perspective on what is authentic, caring actions and what is controlling and manipulative behaviour. If your partner asks where you're going and what time you'll be home, know the difference as to whether or not they are being attentive and curious or controlling.

When it comes to DV know your rights, be informed and acknowledge DV for what it is.

When gaining support from others, look at who can help and who you can talk to; friends and family, support organisations like DV Connect, your local domestic violence support service, Lifeline, the police, the community legal service, a lawyer; these are just some of the areas you may choose to seek help from. By having the support of others, you'll have the courage and strength to change your situation.

If you are experiencing DV, be mindful that the days immediately after you leave the situation are the most dangerous, particularly with regard to separation assault; therefore having an exit strategy is imperative. This means planning things like where you'll go and who can support you prior to actually leaving.

DV does not discriminate. I consider myself a strong, independent women, yet it still affected me. I can't say for how long or even when it started affecting me because I didn't recognise it as abuse.

Since experiencing DV, I've spoken at DV awareness and prevention events. During these events I talk about the 'What, Why and How' as well as the past, present and future, and provide guidance on what to do if DV is affecting your life.

My suggestion to someone who is experiencing a similar DV situation is to consider my 6S six-step approach:

1. SPOT the signs
2. START the change process
3. SEEK support
4. SHARE with others you trust
5. SAFETY and self-care
6. STAND strong

If you've had, or are currently experiencing DV, there are support networks available. See the 'Resources' section at the end of the book for some organisations that may be able to help.

Be safe and stay safe.

Once you're in a safe physical space, you can then address other areas, like your mental space; this is sometimes referred to as mindset.

Moving on with the right mindset

Changing your thoughts and mindset to focus on the positive, or at the very least the potential of the opportunities that now present themselves to you, really is the best strategy to help you move on.

Many references are made about mindset, so what exactly is mindset? I like to describe it as your thoughts and beliefs. I could go into detail about the psychological factors that affect your mindset, like your background, your influences and circumstances, nature versus nurture, community, the people around you and everything in between; each impacting your thoughts and attitude and therefore your mindset. In simple language, one way of finding out your mindset is the 'glass is half full or half empty' question.

I've always had a positive mindset with the 'glass is half full' kinda thinking, though, with my separation that was challenged on so many levels. The good news is that your mindset is what you create it to be.

If you're of the 'glass is half full' school of thought, continuing with your positive mindset will keep you in good stead for your separation journey and know that if you have issues with staying positive, it's completely natural – you are human after all.

If, on the other hand, you are more drawn to the 'glass is half empty' thinking, fear not, as all thoughts with focused attention can become empowering and create a positive attitude. Start to challenge your thinking.

One way to do this is by becoming aware of your Automatic Negative Thoughts (ANTs) and turning them into Performance Enhancing Thoughts (PETs). In short: turn your ANTs into PETs; this is what I focus on with my clients. Another way of looking at it is to adopt a positive perspective, your ability to embrace new thoughts will reap positive results.

Maybe this is a good time to mention that the glass is always full – half with liquid, half with air. Or perhaps the engineer in you may be thinking the glass is twice the size it needs to be! So, with this new information, your multiple-choice question is: How do you see the glass now?

1. half full
2. half empty
3. always full
4. twice the size it needs to be
5. always refillable
6. all of the above
7. something else
8. none of the above!

My point here is that new information is likely to give you a new perspective; what you decide to do with that new information and perspective is up to you. Will it challenge your thinking and subsequently change your behaviour? Or will you stay in your holding pattern? Each decision you make and action you take will ultimately affect your outcomes.

Let me challenge your thinking with a little story of an incident that happened to me whilst I was doing my weekly grocery shopping.

It was late one Wednesday evening and whilst I was looking for toothpaste, I heard two voices coming from the adjacent aisle, the couple's conversation went like this:

Person 1: 'You're not normal, you've never been normal!'

Person 2: 'Like you'd know.'

Person 1: 'Of course I know, I've known you for years.'

Person 2: 'Well it just goes to show you don't know me as well as you thought you did.'

Intrigued, I made my way towards them and as I turned the corner, I could see that they were perusing the bottles of shampoo and conditioners: for dry hair, for oily hair, for normal hair!

While I thought person 1 was calling person 2 crazy, it couldn't have been further from the truth. Existing thoughts and assumptions play a significant part in making sense of our world, our subconscious thoughts determine our interpretations. Here's the good news: we can change them if we want to, we just need to put the effort in.

The first step in any process of change is to *start*. The fact that you are reading this book is a good indication that you are on the verge of change, a change in circumstance and a change in mindset.

Here's one of my personal and most used coaching strategies; it's one of my favourites and I use it almost every day, both personally, professionally and alongside my clients. It's the foundation to help embrace change, I call it the FDC.

Four Decisions of Choice (FDC)

In any given situation, I believe that you have four major decisions, these are:

1. change the situation
2. change the meaning
3. change yourself
4. do nothing

Let's explore each of these in a little more detail:

CHANGE THE SITUATION

Stop or do something different.

In short, take action of a different kind. Get proactive. Start the process of exploring your options. If you are separating, speak with a counsellor, talk with the bank, research lawyers that could help you. Nothing progresses on your terms without action, inspired or otherwise.

CHANGE THE MEANING

Make the experience a learning opportunity.

Consider that everything is for a reason. If something didn't happen as expected maybe it's because there's something better or more appropriate waiting for you. Challenge your assumptions. Sometimes just changing the meaning can make a seemingly uncomfortable situation better. Separating gives you the opportunity to reclaim your independence and challenge your thinking, and presents an opportunity to reassess your current situation and explore your future goals. It marks the start of a new chapter in your life.

On the topic of assumptions, here's a general one of mine: I get angry with 'idiotic' drivers. You know the ones, those who speed like they're the only ones on the road, oblivious to other drivers. Some don't use indicators, some are tailgaters, some are general 'road hogs', and then there are those with their arm hanging out the window, smoking a cigarette (how can you control a car with one hand holding a hot cancer stick? Oh and by the way, if you didn't already know, it's illegal to smoke whilst driving with children in the vehicle (come on people, let common sense prevail!)).

I digress, back to the speeding car. Imagine changing your mindset about that 'idiotic' driver; what if I challenged your assumptions into thinking that there was a pregnant woman in the car already in labour, or someone was having a heart attack in the back seat, or the driver's child had been in an accident and they were rushing to the hospital to be with them, would you think differently then? I would, I do! Now every time I find myself getting agitated, I reflect on the 'what if', and it helps.

This can be used for dealing with your partner's challenging behaviour too. Change the meaning of what triggers a reaction in you and reframe it so that it works to your advantage rather than it pushing your buttons.

When my ex was behaving badly, whether it was ignorance, avoidance or down right bitterness, aggressive texts, non-sensical emails, threats, demands, accusations or guilt trips, I'd reframe it by changing the meaning so that I interpreted it differently. For example, his avoidance is his issue, his anger is a result of his own behaviour and actions, the fact that he was angry or avoidant to something was a reaction that he chose, not a reaction to *me*.

As challenged as I was, I felt empowered that I could separate my life from his and it reinforced my thinking that him leaving the relationship was okay, and his subsequent behaviour confirmed to me that it was the right decision for us not to be together anymore.

I can't affect his reaction, his interpretation is his, just as no one can make you feel a certain way without your permission. I know this is easier said than done, however with practice and effort you will be more aware of your feelings and your subsequent reaction. *You* get to choose, *you* have free will.

Another thought process is to separate the person from the problem. If your ex is behaving badly, say for example, not providing the relevant information like financial statements, or withholding access to the children, realise that the challenge is with the desired outcome, for example, to have the financial information, to spend time with the children. Focus on the overall outcome that you're seeking. Separate your ex from the problem and you'll find your thoughts and emotions will align with the outcome you want.

By focusing your energy and thoughts on what you want, rather than where you are, means you're giving attention to the end result rather than the current situation and this in turn will accelerate the process of reaching your desired outcomes.

CHANGE YOURSELF

Reflect inwards.

Pay attention to how you are feeling and what thoughts are going through your mind. Consider:

- What are my thoughts and feelings about this?
- What does that say about me?
- What thoughts and assumptions did I make about that situation, that behaviour?

Using the general example of a car speeding past me, my initial reaction is to think 'what a tosser, impatient pig', and some other choice words (colourful ones at that; what a bleeping bleep bleep!). However, focusing on the situation and thinking to myself, 'what could I do or how could I think differently to be in a much better mindset?' helps me identify my own personal development opportunities and be empowered by my choice of thought, and my choice of behaviour. I get to choose my own reaction.

This was true of my separation too. Even after counselling my husband left and I started to think things like, 'did I miss something?', 'I should never have gotten married in the first place', 'what a waste of time'. Then I got to thinking, what does this say about me? What changes can I make in my own life, whether it be circumstances, behaviour or goals? I then used the experience to help others. I've always been involved in personal development whether as a global corporate player travelling the world and working insanely long hours, or as a more relaxed free-spirited massage therapist and mindset coach being home-based with essential oils, incense burning and calming music, and by always being an attentive mother educating my children on both the external world around them and their internal world of thoughts and feelings; interpersonal skills and intrapersonal skills.

DO NOTHING

Keep things as they are, accept them and the consequences.

Sometimes doing nothing is the best option. There are instances when your power is in your non-reaction. I say this a lot with my clients, particularly those who are going through a separation and wanting to send texts with colourful content or rising to the bait of their belligerent ex.

Consciously deciding not to act is different from ignorance or avoidance; burying your head in the sand like an ostrich and hoping things will get better or go away is not going to help you progress in a positive way.

I recently found out that the peacock[16] is associated with patience. So, I'd suggest you be a peacock not an ostrich!

The FDC framework is a good coping technique for any situation and when times get tough or when thoughts start to overwhelm (and they will if you're involved in a separation) it can help keep you grounded, help you get focused and help you transition well through the process of change.

Another little tip that works for me is that I now use the following three words in any given situation that makes me feel agitated: 'Rise Above It'. This gives me my power back, without ignoring the event, and turns it into a win. So, the next time your ex does or says something that could set you off, rise above it and feel good knowing you made your own conscious choice of thought and behaviour.

In your separation journey you'll no doubt be reflecting inward a lot; embrace it!

A point to note here, this is not the time to be in 'victim' mode where you think things like, 'they left because of me, I'm a bad parent and partner, it's all my fault!'. These are not words that empower. Replace these words with more positive and empowering reflections like, 'I've got this, I'm a good parent, I have healthy relationships, I'm independent, I've made it this far, I can do this'. You've got this!

By using the FDC framework you can start to change your thinking to a positive mindset and make meaning that aligns with the best version of you.

This type of reframing is so important in the process of life in general and it can be used in any situation, at any time, within any circumstance, for anyone, with anything; now that's a great thing!

So next time you're challenged with something or someone, decide which of the FDCs best fits and implement it.

It's powerful to be in complete control of your thoughts and behaviour. Go you!

6S ACTION points:

Visit www.helenslater.com.au to get your free:

- 6S Behavioural Styles information sheet.
- 6S Four Decisions of Choice (FDC) summary sheet.
- 6S Just separated ACTION points checklist.
- DV resources links.

Website links:

- www.5lovelanguages.com
- www.anrows.org.au/

2
PROPERTY AND MONEY

Understanding it's more than bricks and mortar

- Asset pool: what you own and what you owe
- Division: who gets what
- Financial situation
- Offers of Settlement
- Spousal maintenance

When it comes to property settlement the primary process used was commonly known as the 'Four Step Process', however, due to recent changes it is now known as the 'Five Step Process'.[1]

Here is my definition of The Five Step Process and what's considered:

1. Whether it's appropriate (aka 'just and equitable') to change who has what.
2. The current asset pool.
3. What you each contributed.
4. Your current and future needs.
5. Who gets what: a 'just and equitable' split.

Personally, in keeping with my 6S approach, I like to refer to it in six word; your past, present and future monies.

Now, before you start stressing over how much you'll receive, it's important to know that most people incorrectly assume that whomever brings in the most income from their work gets a bigger share; this is not how it works. For those of you who have been a stay-at-home parent or have been the one maintaining the household on a regular basis, this is taken into consideration.[2] In short, just because one person is out working doesn't automatically mean they get a bigger share of the assets. Let's start at the beginning.

The Five Step Process is broken down into:

Step One: Whether it's appropriate to change who currently has what

Determining whether there's a need to change or adjust the current ownership of assets held by each party, is the purpose of this step, as well as whether there has indeed been a separation in the first place.

It has been suggested that a short-term relationship, considered between three and five years, may have no need for adjustments or a change to the current status of property held by each of the parties, particularly if they have maintained separate finances during the relationship, however, this is unusual and more often than not most property settlement continues through the following four steps.

If you're interested, this is the extra step that changed the Four Step Process to a Five Step Process. Now, onto Step Two.

Step Two: The current asset pool

The aim here is to agree on the asset pool; both assets and liabilities are considered.[3]

Property is the term used for all assets[4] not just bricks and mortar.

In order to divide and agree on property settlement, first the asset pool needs to be agreed upon. This is what both you and your partner have between you, everything from the family home, investment property, cars you drive, money in the bank and in savings, trust accounts, superannuation funds; as well as furniture and personal belongings and collectables that are often referred to as chattels. Basically, it's anything that is worth something financially, from the home you own to the vehicle you drive including any personalised rego plates!

An easy way to remember this is that if you can sell it and get money for it, it goes into the asset pool. Also consider financial aspects like PayPal accounts, loyalty points like flybuys and Air Miles, and anything else of this nature. In addition to assets, anything that has a debt, such as a mortgage and loan repayments gets added as a liability. A small point to note here is that a debt owed by a spouse is also treated as property and in this instance is a liability.[5]

In order to identify the asset pool, you and your ex need to collate and share all relevant financial information with regard to monies and finances, both assets and debts. This part of the legal process is called 'Disclosure'.

Family Law Rule 13.01[6] states that each party to a case has a duty to the court and to each other party to give full and frank disclosure of all information relevant to the case, in a timely manner.

You'll hear the words 'disclosure' and 'discovery', and though these are to achieve the same outcome, the way and means to achieve that outcome are slightly different; here's the difference as I like to describe it:

- **Disclosure** – showing all your information (being proactive).[7]
- **Discovery** – showing information after being asked for it (being reactive).[8]

In other words, you need to provide your ex or the other side with copies of all your financially related documents, this includes (but isn't limited to):

- bank documents (bank and visa statements, loan agreements)
- government documents (Centrelink statements, Parenting Payment correspondence)
- superannuation (yearly statements)
- emails that are relevant to your case (for example, I included emails that identified my foreign currency exchange transfers)
- business interests
- miscellaneous items (any other information you feel is relevant to the matter. In my case it included the accountant's input, the Red Book valuation of vehicles, pet expenses, I even included the lawyers' invoices)

Once you've collated all your information, you'll need to present it in an organised format. See the following example for an idea of how that's done.

Lawyers are regularly collating and presenting this information, usually in lever-arch folders. You'll be charged for their time, the stationery, photocopies of each document, and bear in mind each document is usually copied at least twice (one for your file/the lawyer's file and one for the other side as disclosure). Speak with your lawyer to find out what you can do yourself to reduce your fees.

LIST OF DOCUMENTS AS AT [DATE]

Ref No.	Document	Dated	Owner	Date Disclosed
	Bank Documents			
1	ANZ acct 12341234 Statement	01.01.2020 - 01.03.2020	Joint	
1.1	ANZ acct 12341234 Statement 2	02.03.2020 - 02.06.2020		
2	ANZ Credit Card 12121212 Statement	01.01.2020 - 01.03.2020		
	Government Documents			
3	Confirmation of Intent to Claim	04.04.2020		
4	Letter from Centrelink, Your Parenting Payment	24.04.2020		
5	Letter from Centrelink, Your Centrelink Payment	24.05.2020		
	Superannuation Documents			
6	Sun Super Statement	01.01.2020		
	Emails			
7	Email from XETrade for bid processed $10,000 bought	02.02.2020		
	Miscellaneous			
8	The Red Book pricing authority Subaru	04.05.2020		
9	Expenses for Danny the Dog	undated		
10	Letter from Accountant detailing assets and liabilities	05.06.2020		

You can continue to add to your disclosure documents, just add an additional number after the initial correspondence reference number.

This paperwork can become a significant amount of 'tree destruction', so getting a good supply of paper, tabs and large lever-arched files is a good idea, as you'll probably need them!

Once all the disclosure information is known and received, a summary can be created, usually in a form of a table. Here's one very basic example:

- Column one is the asset or liability **name** (e.g. Vehicle: Subaru Forester).
- Column two shows the **amount** of the asset or liability (e.g. $15,000) (include a minus -$ if it's a debt or liability).
- Column three shows **who owns** the asset or liability (e.g. Joint, or percentage/share).

As in the previous example, some lawyers add an additional column for when the disclosure document was received.

For the purpose of this demonstration I have identified one party as HS (my initials) and the other as EXP (ex/partner), you may want to use the traditional identification of husband and wife if that reflects your circumstances.

ITEM	AMOUNT	OWNERSHIP
Home	$600,000	Joint 50/50
Vehicle: Subaru Forester	$15,000*	HS 100%
Vehicle: Toyota	$25,000*	EXP 100%
ANZ Saving Account	$50,000	Joint 50/50
Q Superannuation	$150,000	EXP 100%
TOTAL:	$840,000	
DEBT/LIABILITIES		
		Joint 50/50
		EXP 100%
TOTAL Assets minus Liabilities:	$487,500	

Notes:

*Redbook Value.

Redbook is a guide for estimating the value of vehicles and commonly used in valuing vehicles in disclosure,[9] you can access it too, at: www.redbook.com.au.

Step Three: What you each contributed

This step is concerned with who brought what into the relationship when you first got together;[10] did you both have nothing, was it a 50/50 match, did one have or contribute more than the other; this can refer to assets like finances, vehicles, property. If you had a property with a large mortgage with little equity then this will not be considered a large contribution but rather a liability as it comes with a debt.

In this context, equity is the difference between the value of the house and the value of the mortgage, for example, let's say you have a home that is worth $500,000 and you still owe $400,000 on your mortgage, the equity therefore is $100,000.

You'll need to consider assets and equity, liabilities and debt.

Your home is an asset, however, your mortgage is a liability. A mortgage is a debt that you owe.[11]

Here's an example, let's say person A comes into the relationship with a $100,000 contribution which is used for home renovations and living expenses, with person B having $15,000 equity in a $450,000 house. Though simplistic figures, you can see that the $100,000 contribution is greater than the $15,000 equity.

An important point to note is that contributions are not based purely on financial aspects, but also incorporates time, parenting and household duties. The three specifics here are:

- financial
- non-financial
- household and parenting

Let's look at these a little more:

Financial

This is quite self-explanatory, these are financial contributions of assets (property, vehicles, etc.) and funds (money, shares, superannuation, inheritances) that make up the asset pool.[12]

Non-financial

This relates to contributions to the acquisition, conservation or improvement of your property.[13] This may relate to genuine home improvements and renovations or to scenarios where there is a dominant homemaker, or stay-at-home-parent that allows the other to focus 100% on making money and increasing the property pool.

Household and Parenting

This component relates to the welfare of the family unit, your immediate family, and your role as homemaker and/or parent; male or female, it makes no difference.[14]

Some examples of the homemaker role are: cooking, cleaning, home maintenance and childcare.

Step Four: Your current and future needs

These relate to Step Four in the Five Step Process namely; future needs, resources and potential adjustments.[15]

After looking at past contributions, attention is now given to future needs of both parties, resources and subsequently any potential adjustments. Some of these are:

- age and health[16]
- income, property, financial resources and capacity to work[17]
- care of child(ren)[18]
- supporting themselves (you)[19]

- supporting another[20]
- pension and/or superannuation entitlements[21]
- standard of living that is reasonable in the circumstances[22]
- earning capacity (by attending a course of education or training or establishing a business or otherwise to obtain an adequate income)[23]
- duration of the marriage and how that has affected earning capacity[24]
- the need to protect a party who wishes to continue the role as a parent[25]
- financial circumstances of cohabiting with another person[26]
- child support payable[27]
- any other circumstances the court considers relevant[28]
- terms of any Binding Financial Agreement (BFA)[29]

For full and comprehensive details of the exact information, there's a link on my website (www.helenslater.com.au).

Consideration to future needs is when potential adjustments are identified. These are usually made as a percentage (for example, 10%-15% adjustment for being the primary carer, 5%-10% due to limited earning capacity to reiterate, these are simple examples only). These adjustments are then added as an overall percentage and calculated into the contributions step figure. For example, a 60/40 split in favour of person A, with a 15% adjustment for future needs becomes a 75/25 split, or if in the favour of person B, becomes a 45/55 split. Make sense?

Let's keep it simple, if you start at a 50/50 split and person A has an adjustment of 10% for future needs, the split figure becomes 60/40 in favour of person A.

Person A

Their contributions are determined as 50%.

Their future needs determined at an additional 10%.

Their total percentage becomes 60%.

Person B

Their contributions are determined as 50%.

Because of person A's future needs, there is an adjustment of 10%.

Their total percentage becomes 40%.

In my case I gained adjustments to the percentage in my favour as I had brought the bigger contribution into the relationship, additionally I wasn't receiving any significant child support and I was the primary carer. I lived alone with two young children, with significant travel time between home and childcare. Plus, I was able to identify my ex's wanton and wasteful behaviour from his self-taught share-trading activity, losing up to $40,000 in one day's transaction (even writing that takes my breath away), he also transferred significant monies from our joint account without my knowledge. Three days before our first court attendance, after finally getting his disclosure, I found out that from the $250k+ balance, the majority was gone! (Breathe!)

Though extremely rare, I was able to argue what's called the Kowaliw v Kowaliw principle.[30] Key words: recklessly, negligently or wantonly. In my language: incompetence and poor investment decisions (all without my knowledge or permission).

The reason it's so rare is that losses are usually worn equally in a relationship whether from gambling and the pokies, to poor decision making in business and investments.

'...in the words of Justice Baker: "financial loss incurred by the parties in the course of the marriage ... should be shared by them (although not necessarily equally) except in the following circumstances:

i. where one of the parties has embarked upon a course of conduct designed to reduce or minimise the effective value or worth of matrimonial assets; or

ii. **where one of the parties has acted recklessly, negligently or wantonly with matrimonial assets, the overall effect of which has reduced or minimised their value.**'[31]

Another aspect here is called Add Back.[32] Add Back refers to assets and monies that one of the parties dispose of soon after separation, whether that's selling something of value at a significantly reduced price, to indulging in expensive holidays or buying the new partner an expensive engagement ring! Add Back is complicated and requires disclosure of the disposal of, or sale of, assets within 12 months prior to separation. Ideally the Add Back is added back into the overall asset pool (usually to become part of the 'disposing' person's split). Though it didn't really help my case as, ironically, due to my ex's reckless behaviour there was so little left to split! Grrrrr, let's move on...

Some of you may be thinking about spousal maintenance and where that fits in, I'll share more on that a little later, for now here is a super quick definition of the difference between spousal maintenance and property settlement as I understand it:

- **Spousal maintenance** – usually short-term financial needs, paid regularly over an agreed timeframe, or in a lump sum, depending on circumstances.
- **Future Needs step** – long-term needs and resources of each of you.

Step Five: Who gets what: a just and equitable split

By this step you should have:

1. agreement on what is in the asset pool
2. confirmed who brought what into the relationship
3. identified what each of you need

Step five is about reviewing the whole picture to make sure the division is just and equitable, making sure there is a balance in the distribution of assets. Let's call it a 'birds eye view' to see the whole picture of who's to have what now, and what's been considered in provisions for the future, then based on that to make sure an appropriate settlement is received.

This is such a grey area as there are no hard and fast rules; the Judge will be using their knowledge of the process to 'tick the box' on the final division of assets. There's a discretionary element here which basically means it's not as clear as black and white, and whilst one person or lawyer may consider XX/XX the best result, the other side may not; this goes for the reviewing Judge too. Whilst reviewing the proposed division of assets, the Judge considers all of the factors[33] and the subsequent adjustments; they'll be looking for an equitable balance in the asset distribution, making sure one party isn't dominating the split unless there are specific circumstances and factors to consider. This was the case for my matter. Here's an insight into my property settlement; grab a coffee or wine, and get comfortable…

The day my property settlement was heard and finalised by the Judge was totally unexpected, both to me and the other side.

It had been eleven months since my first court attendance and I was still awaiting full disclosure and discovery from my ex. He and his solicitor were not forthcoming with the relevant documents, dragging their heels so much so that at my request they were eventually court-ordered to provide disclosure within a fourteen-day timeframe of all my ex's information, including his Trust account with the law firm. Here we were months later and I'd still not received anything. On this particular day in court I was hoping to get that disclosure, or if not, seek some sort of penalty for breaching the court order, particularly as the law firm could, and should, have sent their Trust account information for my ex's matter as it did not require any input from him whatsoever.

A point to note here, this highlights how some lawyers are inefficient or ineffective in their dealings, and why it's imperative you do your research and get a lawyer that has your best interests and your back, as well as being compliant within the law.

Perhaps this is a good time to point out that as I was a self-represented litigant, the solicitor acting for my ex appeared to use this as an excuse to act with ignorance, avoidance and bullying; not replying to any of my emails for over four months even those including offers of settlement (more on this later) and when I did receive a reply it was rude, insulting and with elements of intimidation and bullying.

I took those emails to other lawyers to get their feedback on the situation and the conduct of my ex's solicitor, and they were all of the same opinion: the conduct was unprofessional and unethical and that I had a good case to report them to the Legal Services Commission – the professional body that makes sure lawyers are behaving properly.

The solicitor's behaviour and conduct was extremely unprofessional, not only were there delays in correspondence and the process, but the language and intimidation in communication was also evident, including one instance outside the courtroom when my ex's solicitor not only attempted to bully me into agreeing to their terms, but also changed the figures on the paperwork of our property settlement division, giving the impression that I'd signed off on it!

I'd arrived early at court and was able to accommodate one of the small rooms in the courthouse. I settled in for the day, this way I could prepare and stay calm (well as calm as you can be when getting ready to stand before a Judge), when in walks my ex's solicitor to 'negotiate'. The solicitor stood over me and said that he knew the Judge very well, and that the outcome wouldn't be good for me if I didn't agree, that I'd better be ready and know the law! It's fair to say that I was intimidated, however, I didn't let the solicitor know that, and I slowly yet purposefully stood up, looked him directly in the eyes and said, 'we'll see'; he promptly left the room. I sat down with my heart racing.

Eventually our matter was called, and we were before the Judge. Fortunately, I was able to raise the bullying, intimidation and figure 'tampering' with the Judge and this raised his eyebrows and resulted in a few choice questions for the other side. Apologies from the solicitor followed, and some feeble excuse of a misunderstanding.

Another small point to note, this particular solicitor also pushed passed me on the way into the courtroom and positioned themselves in my position at the bar table; typically, the Applicant stands on the right, left to the Judge, the Respondent on the left, right to the Judge. When I approached him to say he was in my place, he replied curtly with 'this is the position for qualified solicitors'! I didn't want to cause a scene, so I took my place at the Respondent's table. Fortunately, this did not affect my case, in fact, the Judge was very sympathetic to my situation, and granted me everything that I asked for, including a couple of trial dates, to which the other side argued against, without success. Result, sort of!

It's very unlikely that you will encounter such poor ethics and lack of professionalism and end up lodging a complaint; just because your lawyer doesn't return your calls or reply to your emails as quickly as you would like them to is not a reason to go knocking on the door of the Legal Services Commission. However, if you have good reason to believe that the conduct of your lawyer, or the solicitor representing your ex, constitutes a complaint, then approach the Legal Services Commission to seek further clarity and assistance.

Most lawyers and law firms are more than happy to discuss any concerns you have about your matter, whether it's about their business or the other side.

Offers of settlement

Any time during legal proceedings you can make an offer of settlement.

An offer of settlement is exactly that, an offer to your ex-partner outlining who's to get what, in order to finalise legal proceedings. It outlines what property each of you will receive or retain. An offer can also include children's arrangements.

I presented more than generous offers of settlement on numerous occasions as I just wanted legal proceedings over. At the time, offering my ex significantly more than what he was entitled to was worth it just to release the hassle and stress of court and all the associated costs; in my mind (and backed-up by some lawyers' input) the idea of offering him money and assets to bring proceedings to a halt meant I would be saving legal costs both in the short term and the long term.

It was a bit of a 'rock and a hard place' dilemma; give him money so that we could cease legal proceedings and move on with our lives, or continue putting energy, time and money into legal fees and court costs to get a 'just' settlement that wasn't guaranteed.

Disappointingly, he and his solicitor rejected my first offer, and additional offers weren't even acknowledged, not even the courtesy of a reply; as previously mentioned, disgusting behaviour on the part of my ex's solicitor. That said, please note that you will not usually get an answer straight away, all my offers of settlement were given with a fourteen-day timeframe.

During my matter, when the time came to ask for what I was seeking, I told the presiding Judge, 'the lot, your Honour', which at the time wasn't very much. The Judge explained that wasn't going to happen and proceeded to explain why (remember 'just and equitable' Step Four). I then explained that I felt a 75/25 split in my favour was 'fair' (fair is a word that is not typically used in court, as it is just too subjective, that said, the Judge agreed to hear what I had to say) and based on my 'submissions', agreed.

Subsequently, based on my background information on the Kowaliw v Kowaliw[34] principle and Add Back argument, as well as my ex having two vehicles, both substantially worth more than my clapped-out old banger of a car whose boot door had to be held up with a broom handle when getting the double stroller or groceries out of the back, the Judge agreed to an adjustment.

The Judge then asked for any additional information; this is when I requested an adjustment due to lack of child support, the Judge agreed, and an additional adjustment was made, finally taking it to 85/15 split. I just wanted the matter over and with that I decided to let my ex keep whatever he had in his possession at the time, which according to his limited disclosure was two vehicles, his Super and next to nothing in the bank. I have no idea if he hid any money, I could have used the services of a forensic accountant if I wanted to find out but, in all honesty, I didn't want to spend a dollar more. I just wanted out of the court system and to start my life anew.

You can do your property settlement and division without lawyers, though in my opinion you really need to be amicable and in a good place to do that. You can seek the support of experienced accountants or mediators, and get it signed off with the court. I tried so hard to stay out of court, yet my ex was just too avoidant and vague, and with him holding all the money and assets, seeking the court's assistance really was the only way to progress with some kind of momentum.

Spousal Maintenance

Spousal maintenance can be a touchy subject for most people.

It's not like it is in the movies. The reality is that when you physically and emotionally separate it has a knock-on effect on your financial situation and income.

Subsequently, as you're no longer sharing income from, or with, your ex, you may find yourself in a position where you need to seek spousal maintenance to assist you to support yourself financially and to get back on track.

Spousal maintenance is considered a stepping stone, it's not a means to receive income on an indefinite basis. It's time-framed, with either regular payments, say, over two or three years, or as a lump sum, intended to assist you financially and help you rebuild your life to be independent.

Ultimately, it's short-term financial support. It's income when you don't have any other source of revenue, no job, no passive income or no investment returns. Whether or not you or your ex are entitled to spousal maintenance depends on each of your circumstances, let's break it down into, yes, you've guessed it, six aspects:

1. Yours and your ex's age and health.
2. Yours and your ex's income, property and financial resources.
3. Yours and your ex's ability to work.
4. If the marriage affected yours or ex's ability to work.

5. What's considered a suitable standard of living.
6. If there are children, and with whom the children live.

Obviously, it goes without saying (yet here I am saying it) the court will consider the needs of the applicant (the person seeking spousal maintenance) as well as the respondent's capacity to pay.

Some actions you can do immediately are:

Get your affairs in order, now! All your paperwork, from your Will to your bank accounts, passwords to Superannuation. If you have a joint bank account, make sure you contact the bank and request two signatures are always needed from this point onwards. And set up your own individual bank account.

Start a journal to keep a record of events, dates, times and what happened. This may become very important later on, particularly when dealing with the details of events for when you need to complete affidavits and evidence (if this is required of you).

Make a note or at least agree on your separation date.

Create a new personal email account.

Consider what you write. From this point onwards bear in mind that what, and how, you communicate now may eventually be read or seen by a Judge; this includes social media content. I have seen some cases where one of the parties' communication has turned a case.

Stay grounded. Release stress. Breathe.

Everyone experiences stress in their life at some point, and going through a relationship break up is one of the most stressful times you'll get to experience. Knowing how to reduce stress can help you stay healthy; physically, mentally and emotionally.

Consider what you like and build on that. Here's some pointers on what may work for you:

- Avoid procrastination by being proactive, e.g. prioritise, focus and take action
- Breathe deeply
- Chew gum (one study showed it to reduce stress by creating brainwaves that are similar to that of a relaxed person, it also increases blood flow to the brain…..yep, this one surprised me too!)
- Create a 'vision-board' of your ideal things, cut out magazine pictures or words and collate them in a folder or pin them to a corkboard (that's what I do) and review regularly
- Daydream (let your thoughts wander)
- Eat well (and probably best to limit alcohol)
- Exercise (no need to purchase gym membership just yet, a walk can work wonders)
- Focus on the positive, e.g. affirm, reframe, (gratitude all the way)
- Have a massage
- Hug (physical contact releases oxytocin the body's very own feel good drug)
- Laugh (my second personal favourite)

- Listen to soothing music or vibes that make you feel good (my personal favourite)
- Meditate
- Organise; your space (declutter), your thoughts (journal), your tasks (to-do lists)
- Practice mindfulness; be present in the moment (whether quietly at home with a scented candle or out and about soaking up the sun, feeling the refreshing rain, embracing the chaos/noise of the outside world)
- Read (get lost in a book)
- Say 'no' (learning to say 'no' can be a learning curve yet once you've experimented with it, the easier it'll be)
- Spend time with friends/family (those that you're happiest around)
- Take time out, guilt free (e.g. watch a movie, go to a café and people watch, enjoy a bubble bath)
- Talk with someone, whether a trusted friend or an experienced professional
- Use essential oils
- Write things down
- Practice yoga

In summary be active, take control, connect with others and have some guilt free 'me' time.

Now to the practicalities of 'disclosure'. Start to collate all your related paperwork and documents, here's a list of what to include:

- bank statements
- credit card statements
- earnings (e.g. payslips) and any other financial resources
- Centrelink statements and letters
- shares and dividend statements
- trust account statements
- superannuation statements
- insurance policies
- vehicle registration documents
- house title deeds
- lease agreements
- company/partnership documents

I also created an 'All Important Documents and Info Folder' (you'll be needing copies of some of these documents to present to your lawyer); I suggest you create one of your own and include documents such as:

- passports
- birth certificate
- marriage certificate
- your will and Enduring Power of Attorney
- ownership of home documents (certificate of title) and/or rental lease agreements
- citizenship certificate, immigration certificates or visas

Alongside copies of your:

- driving licence
- important cards like medicare or credit cards
- superannuation statements
- tax returns
- AEC information

It's also useful to have details of your usernames and passwords.

After my legal proceedings mine also included:

- divorce decree (certificate of divorce)
- change of name documents
- final court orders
- protection order

6S ACTION points:

Visit www.helenslater.com.au to get your free:

- 6S Five Step Process summary sheet.
- 6S Tips on how to reduce stress.
- 6S Checklist of important documents.

Website links:

- www5.austlii.edu.au/au/legis/cth/consol_act/fla1975114/s75.html
- www.familycourt.gov.au/wps/wcm/connect/fcoaweb/

family-law-matters/property-and-finance/maintenance/spousal-maintenance

3
CHILDREN AND PARENTING

Priority number one: what's in the best interest of the children?

Love your children more than you despise each other. Remember, it's about progression of a child not *possession* of a child.

- Parental Responsibility

  - Equal Shared Parental Responsibility
  - Sole Parental Responsibility

- Parenting Plans, Consent Orders and Parenting Orders
- Parenting Tips
- Independent Children's Lawyer (ICL)
- Family Consultant/Family Report Writer

- Child Support

Remember, it's you who is separating from your partner, not the children (unless of course there is domestic violence).

Parental Responsibility

By default, parental responsibility is usually shared equally and identified as equal shared parental responsibility, unless there is an order for sole parental responsibility.[1]

Equal Shared Parental Responsibility

Equal shared parental responsibility means both parties are responsible for *decisions* relating to the child, not to be confused with equal time with the child.[2]

Parental responsibility is about the child's best interests and includes short-term decisions like what they eat, what they wear and their day-to-day activities, as well as long-term decisions such as the schools they attend, where they live, religious upbringing and health matters. If each party is spending time with the child, then the day-to-day decisions of the child falls with the person who has the child in their care at the time.[3]

Sole Parental Responsibility

Sole parental responsibility means one parent is solely responsible for the major decisions of the child. Sole parental responsibility is a decision of the court, it's uncommon and seldom granted. I'd summarise it like this: sole parental responsibility is usually granted when one parent is bad, mad or sad. For example, in jail, where there are DV issues, is suffering serious mental health issues, or is deceased! I'm sure if you asked a lawyer or Judge they would have a good long list of the reasons why sole parental responsibility is granted, but I like to keep my stuff simple.

In summary:

- **Equal Shared Parental Responsibility** – default of the court, equal decision making on short-term and long-term decisions; having good levels of communication between the two parents.
- **Sole Parental Responsibility** – seldom granted, sole decision making, particularly on long-term decisions. Communication is dysfunctional and there is a high level of conflict.

How a court determines what is in a child's best interests.

The two primary considerations here are:

1. The benefit to the child of having a meaningful relationship with both of the child's parents.[4]

2. The need to protect the child from physical or psychological harm from being subjected to, or exposed to, abuse, neglect or family violence.[5]

Additional considerations include:

- Views of the child (with emphasis on their maturity and level of understanding. The views of an eight-year-old will more than likely be different to that of a thirteen-year-old, considering that they have a good understanding of the situation. Also be mindful that some children may feel conflicted and not want to impact either parent in a negative way, for example they may express a desire to live with both parents).[6]
- The child's relationship with both parents and extended family, such grandparents, siblings, step-siblings, aunties, uncles. (Bear in mind that sometimes love can be greater than DNA.)[7]
- The effect change in circumstances may have on the child.[8]
- The extent to which each parent has taken the opportunity to actually parent, in short, participation in making decisions, spending time with the child, and regular communication.[9]
- The practical difficulties and expense of the child spending time with either parent. As an example, think relocation and the subsequent challenges this presents.[10]
- The extent to which the parents have actually paid for

the child. Financial contributions, including payment of child support.[11]
- The capacity of both parents to provide for the needs of the child. This includes not just time, place and money, but also other needs like emotional and mental needs.[12]
- If the child is an Aboriginal or Torres Strait Islander child, their right to enjoy their culture.[13]
- Family Violence.[14]
- Any other fact or circumstance the court thinks is relevant.[15]

All these points are taken into consideration as the Judge doesn't know you, your partner or the children, and having guidelines like these assists the court in making orders that are in the best interest of the children.

Now let's look at Parenting Plans, Consent Orders and Parenting Orders.

Parenting Plan versus **Consent Order** versus **Parenting Order;** what's what?

A simple description of each in one sentence:

- **Parenting Plan** – A signed agreement between both parties, which is not legally binding, though would likely be influential in any future court proceedings.[16]

- **Consent Orders** – Legally binding Family Court orders which are agreed in advance by the parties.[17]
- **Parenting Orders** – Interim or final orders made by the Family Court after submissions and hearings.[18]

Now with the general gist, let's dive in a little deeper.

A **Parenting Plan** is a written agreement signed and dated by the parties in relation to arrangements for the children. You can do this yourselves or with the help of a counsellor, family dispute resolution practitioner (FDRP) or lawyers.

It is not approved or filed with the court.

It is not legally binding.

It is however a guide to expectations and a clear understanding of the: when (dates), what (changeovers, events, etc.) and where (location) details. A parenting plan will supersede any previous arrangements, even earlier court orders.

Centrelink and the Child Support Agency can use a parenting plan to assist them in any related calculations and/or benefits that are appropriate to your situation.

A **Consent Order** is an agreement between the parties.

You do not need to attend court.

It is approved by the court.

It is legally binding and enforceable, therefore, there are consequences for breaching it.

A **Parenting Order** is made by the court after submissions and hearings. First you need to complete an Initiating Application and then attend court.

It is approved by the court.

It is legally binding and enforceable, therefore, there are consequences for breaching it.

If you or your ex breach a legally binding order without a specific reason or reasonable excuse, then a Contravention order can be sought by the other parent.

A Contravention order is used to seek an order from the court to impose a punishment or consequence on a person for breaching a court order.

Before filing an application for a Contravention order, you should consider the outcome you want. Remedies from the court range from the enforcement of an order to punishment for failing to obey an order[19] see chapter four for more information.

An Application in a Case may be a better way to go rather than a Contravention order, particularly if you don't want to punish your ex. More on an this a little later.

Back to Parenting Plans, if you're wondering what should be included in a Parenting Plan, here's some pointers:

- Who the child will live with.
- How the parents will share day to day parental

responsibilities and make decisions for and about the child.
- How much time the child will spend with each parent.
- A parenting time schedule that shows when each parent has the child.
- How the child will communicate with a parent they do not live with.
- How the parents will communicate about the child.
- What time the child will spend with other people (grandparents, siblings, other relatives).
- How the child will keep in touch with other people when the child is with each parent.
- Arrangements for holidays, birthdays, school breaks, and other special occasions such as Mother's Day or Father's Day.
- What activities each parent will do with the child and who will attend the child's important events.
- A process for making changes to the plan as the child's needs change.
- A method for resolving disputes or a way to solve problems that arise.
- Financial arrangements for the child which can only be included in a parenting plan not a consent order.
- Special provisions and stipulations about how the parents will provide and care for the child.
- Any other aspect of the care, welfare, or development of the child.

There's a lot of information out there that can help you with your parenting plan; Google 'parenting plan' and you'll get results from both The Family Court and The Federal Circuit Court as well as the Attorney General's office, family law firms, Relationships Australia and resourceful Facebook groups.

One of my personal favourite Facebook groups is *'Beanstalk Mums - support and inspiration for single mums'*, where you can access informative blogs, podcasts and join a closed Facebook group to help you with your separation and parenting journey. Sharing regular content that inspires and motivates as well as practical support, all delivered in a positive environment with humour. They have it all, I mean, one of the taglines is 'from solicitors to sex toys', so I think it's fair to say that's a pretty broad base!

And in the spirit of full disclosure, at the time of writing I am one of the Beanstalk Mum advisors (I'm the life coach, and just for the record, I am not associated with the sex toys section in any way, although adding 'sex therapist' to my repertoire of services may be a good way to go?)!

In all seriousness though, if you and your partner are having challenges in your sex life it might be advantageous to seek the support of a sex therapist/sexologist. Imagine avoiding all the stress, legal costs, solicitor meetings, and potential court attendance by addressing intimacy issues; certainly something worth thinking about?! Remember, sex is what lead to this topic of 'parenting' in the first place; we all know where babies come from, right? Whether you're in a same-sex relationship or not, intimacy plays a big part in your continuing relationship (perhaps, highlight that preceding sentence, bookmark this page, and leave it open where your partner can see it. Just a thought. After all, awareness is key, remember, you can't address issues that you don't acknowledge or that you're not aware of: it's back to steps one and two of my six-step model for change: step one – acceptance, step two – awareness).

Okay, enough of the sex talk. More on Parenting Plans and what to include.

What should you keep in mind when making your Parenting Plan, you ask?

When making a parenting plan you should consider the following from the *Family Law Act* (section 63C);[20]

- A parenting plan is all about children arrangements, it doesn't include information about how you and you ex will divide up your assets (this is called a Property Settlement).
- As circumstances change, you may need to revise your plan to meet the needs of your child.
- Your parenting plan should be **in writing, signed and dated by both parents**. It should also be made free from any threat, pressure, or coercion.
- A parenting plan is not legally enforceable, but if both parents agree on the arrangements you can submit your plan to the Family Court and the details of your plan

will then be put into a parenting order (which is legally binding and enforceable).
- You can change your plan at any time by writing out a new plan with your ex, make sure both of you sign it.
- You can change your parenting order by writing out a new parenting plan and submitting it to the court.
- The law presumes that it is in the best interest of the child for both parents to have equal shared parental responsibility (as previously mentioned this does not mean that the child spends equal time with both parents).[21]

Your parenting plan should be unique to your situation and focus on what is best for your children. If age appropriate, you can consider finding out some of your child's living preferences and putting them in the plan if you think it is appropriate.

Keep your plan practical, simple, and as concrete as possible so that you and your ex fully understand it.

Remember the higher the conflict, the more specific you should be in your parenting plan.

Whether you're considering a parenting plan, consent orders or a parenting order, here's what The Family Court states:

What do you need to consider when making parenting arrangements for your child/ren?

Every family is different, so the arrangements that work for your family may be different from other families. Try to make arrangements that will work the best for your child/ren.

When making arrangements for your child/ren, you will need to consider:

- *the age of the child/ren which is very important in deciding what arrangements will work;*
- *establishing a regular routine so the child/ren know the routine and what to expect when, but also be flexible when required;*
- *giving plenty of notice if you wish to change the routine, for example, for special family occasions;*
- *whether it is reasonably practical for the child/ren to spend equal time or substantial and significant time with each parent (substantial and significant time includes weekends, school holidays and days other than those);*
- *how their time will be spent with other significant persons in their lives, such as grandparents and other relatives;*
- *who will look after them after school and where will they spend holidays;*
- *any other things such as choice of school, health care, sport, or religious matters, and;*
- *how to ensure that the child/ren continue to enjoy their culture.*[22]

Another interesting topic to consider is the 'fun parent' or 'Disney Dads'. The court does not like the idea of one parent being the fun parent. The legal definition of a 'Disney Parent' is 'a noncustodial parent who indulges his or her child with gifts and good times during visitation and leaves most or all disciplinary responsibilities to the other parent.' I experienced this first-hand.

When I was going through my legal proceedings my ex spent less time with our children, yet more money on them; ironically it was our joint money that he had transferred, without my knowledge, into his own bank account and his share trading account, both of which I could not access. And, as previously mentioned, he refused to pay child support.

After originally renting an apartment by the beach, he upgraded by renting a modern, detached, two level, four-bedroom house with modern features including pool and spa; all with our joint funds and all just for him (he seldom spent time with our children).

He didn't have a job, he wasn't making any money, yet he was living a lifestyle that was contrary to this. The only reason he could afford the high rent and a 'relaxed' lifestyle was due to him using our joint funds; this was one of his decisions that had a significantly negative impact on our joint finances, namely, he was depleting the asset pool.

Conversely, I was renting an older property, 70s I think, it was a modest three bedroom place without aircon (and on the day I moved in, the temperature was 40 degrees centigrade (for those of you who, like me, are the Fahrenheit generation, that's 104 degrees!) and I can tell you I was thinking, *oh my goodness, what have I done, no aircon*?), nor did it have any modern features, it was almost half the rent that my ex was paying, and yet I had the children the majority of the time.

How do I know what my ex was paying? Well, I saw the same rental listing of the property and I was very keen until I read the rent cost and realised it was outside of my budget, *big time*. Seems my ex thought nothing of the expense, which is probably why we were in the financial predicament we were in, both at the time and during our marriage, as previously mentioned, I relinquished all my financial responsibility to him: big mistake, huge! Always, and I mean ALWAYS, have a bank account in your name only and make regular payments into it, you just never know when you'll need to have access to your own funds. Please remember though this will form part of the relationship property pool. I've heard of people hiding this kind of money, or not disclosing it, and getting away with it. A reminder that to not disclose it is illegal as all assets in existence at the time of separation are required to be disclosed.

Just as a side note, if you're seeking some simple yet effective financial insights, may I suggest Scott Pape's *The Barefoot Investor* (sounds like I'm a waiter enticing you with a smorgasbord of food and wine; I'd suggest The Barefoot Investor books, with a side order of independent finances, followed by regular financial goal planning, and for dessert, join the Barefoot community!). If and when you read Scott's books, I'd like to think you'd see similarities in the way we write; aka educational, conversational, over dinner!

I digress, back to my ex and his spending of joint funds without my knowledge or consent. How could he get away with this? I talked with a solicitor about it, they explained there was nothing I could really do at that stage, so I decided to address it head on, face-to-face.

When I spoke with my ex and raised the discrepancy in his rent costs compared to mine his response was to smile, snigger and walk away; nothing changed. This behaviour was turning out to be his usual response to most things, whether it was talking about parenting arrangements or property settlement, it was truly frustrating.

Though I was regularly frustrated with his usual 'modus operandi' of communication, I talked with him as an adult, both face-to-face and via email; he on the other hand took the stance of a spoilt child or an authoritarian parent. Things like 'you do this or I'll do that', lots of blaming, belittling and control (remember the points of domestic violence in chapter two).

This way of communicating and social interaction is typical of what's called Transactional Analysis. Let me explain a little more on this, and bear with me here, it's not as complex as it sounds.

Transactional Analysis

I encountered Transactional Analysis in the early 90s and even though it sounds like something that belongs in a psychotherapist's office, it's actually a very simple yet effective framework to keep in mind when communicating with others, whether that's your ex, your lawyer, the Judge, your children, your family, friends or peers.

Transactional Analysis was developed by Eric Berne (circa 1961) and in 1964 he wrote a book called *'Games People Play'* which was written in simple language that avoided jargon; it ultimately became a best seller[23].

Here's my simple six-step summary of Transactional Analysis:

1. It's a theory of personality.
2. We have three separate ways of thinking, feeling and reacting to events which is based on our experiences and beliefs, formed since childhood.
3. The three ways are called Parent ego, Adult ego and Child ego.
4. The Parent ego is nurturing or controlling.
5. The Adult ego is logical and natural.
6. The Child ego is free and/or adapted and represents actual thoughts, feelings and reactions.

This analysis of the way people communicate and interact with each other is particularly effective when applied to parenting and negotiating agreements with your ex, and indeed your children.

Transactional Analysis

P = Parent   **A** = Adult   **C** = Child

P	P	P	P	P	P
A	A	A	A	A	A
C	C	C	C	C	C

Complimentary   Crossed   Complimentary

Here are some examples to help illustrate the idea.

Question: When would you like to spend time with the children?

(Adult to Adult)

Response: From Thursday to Monday every other week would work best for me.

(Adult to Adult)

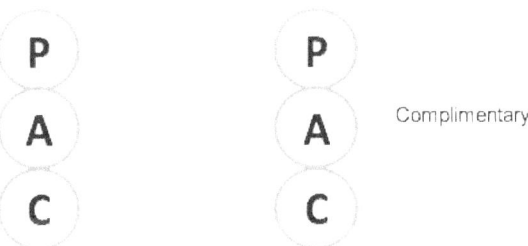

Question: When would you like to spend time with the children?

(Adult to Adult)

Response: Why am I expected to come up with an answer, why can't you do it?

(Child to Parent)

(Or in my case, my ex's ignorance and avoidance, i.e. just ignoring and avoiding answering the question altogether!)

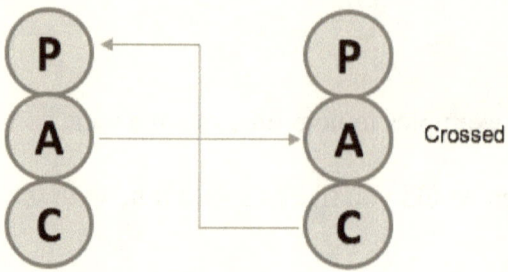

Question: When would you like to spend time with the children?

(Adult to Adult)

Response: You think you know best, you tell me, since you initiated this.

(Parent to Child)

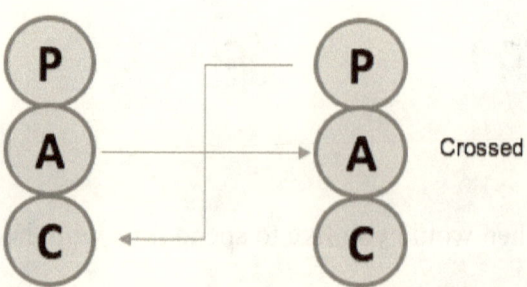

Question: I'm confused, I just don't know when you want to spend time with the children.

(Child to Parent)

Response: Okay, just give me some time to think about it and I'll get back to you.

(Parent to Child)

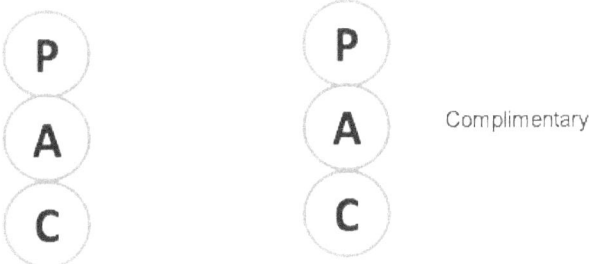

By having 'complimentary' exchanges you can create conversations that are healthy and solution focused, rather than ignorant, avoidant and focused on blame.

Parenting Tips

As parenting is such a huge topic, I'm going to keep it simple with some key points for consideration. Here's my top six:

1. Remember the love languages outlined in chapter one? Consider these when dealing with both your ex and the children;

being relatable and aligned with what their desires are will always give you a more positive outcome.

2. Bear in mind the behavioural styles, these were also outlined in chapter one, again, communicating and behaving in a way that resonates with them, will contribute to getting the best out of the situation.

3. Focus on the outcome you are wanting, adapt where appropriate and use positive language or reframe it. Keep positive as we attract what we focus on (plus the brain doesn't recognise the word 'don't': 'Don't think about pink flying elephants'; bet you saw some pink Dumbos). I regularly speak with stressed parents about their communication with their children, helping them reframe their words so that they focus on the positive and get the result they really want. Some examples are:

> 'Don't run' reframed to 'walk please'.
> 'Don't shout' reframed to 'quiet voices please'.
> 'Don't push your sister' reframed to 'be nice to your sister'.
> Same applies in the context of 'adult' conversation; keep it positive and outcome-focused. Don't use 'don't (doh, I just did!).

4. Set boundaries for the children, your ex and yourself, this includes 'me time' and self-care, and includes perimeters for

friends and family (not always a welcome response by those who want to support you!).

5. Be honest with yourself, the children and, where appropriate, your ex; be mindful of situations where honesty may not be the best approach and adapt accordingly; this doesn't mean lying, it's more about content and context.

6. Consider how the future will look, small stepping-stones of action will help you get there in a more constructive way. After all, action determines outcomes.

Independent Children's Lawyer

An Independent Children's Lawyer (ICL) may be appointed to your matter, the role of the ICL can be found in Section 68LA(S) of the Family Law Act.[24]

Their role is predominately about forming an independent view, based on the evidence available to them, of what is in the best interests of the child, and act in relation to the proceedings in what they believe to be the best interests of the child.[25] This is not to be confused with being the child's independent lawyer. I'm going to repeat that...an independent children's lawyer is not the child's legal representative.

Family Consultant/Family Report Writer

During your parenting negotiations you may have a meeting or interview with a family consultant whose role it is to make recommendations for parenting arrangements; this is known as a family report.[26]

A family report writer is usually a registered psychologist or social worker, who meets with you, your ex and the children, with the purpose of getting an understanding of who you are, your personal values, past circumstances, the current situation and past and present interactions including home life. They may also speak with grandparents, new partners, the ICL, and anyone else who has a significant relationship or role in the lives of the child.[27]

From the information gathered by the family report writer, and based on the interaction between you and them, you and the child, and you and your ex, they consider and suggest what would be in the best interest of the child. As a heads-up, they'll be observing you as soon as you enter the premises, including how you behave around your ex and your interactions in the waiting room.

You usually attend their office, however, I know of some that do home visits which gives them more insight into the current living environment; same rules apply.

They report their findings to the court, in a written family report including their recommendations on where the child should live, with who, and when they should be spending time with each parent.[28]

The day before we were to meet with the family report writer was one of the most challenging days of my life! I remember how emotional and anxious I was, one stand-out moment was immediately after I had put the children to bed. We'd been talking about going on a little road trip in the morning (the family consultant's office was in Brisbane); Brisbane was an hour and a half drive for us, and I wanted to make it a fun event; I packed a 'travel bag' of fun things from snacks to games. After the children had settled for the night, I had a shower and whilst in the shower I was so overwhelmed I just slid to my knees and ended up in the foetal position sobbing.

How could it have gotten to this? I had given my best to enable a smooth transition for the children through our separation and asked my ex so many times (thirty plus) what he wanted in the way of children arrangements (six months later, still no answer). I'd stayed child focused and all I was seeking was an understanding of his expectation of his time with the children; he avoided and ignored the question altogether. And now we were meeting with a family report writer who would speak with each of us for an hour or so and based on that, make a recommendation on where, with whom, and how, the children should live, up until the age of 18 when they become adults. Could my ex not see how awful this predicament was? If only he had expressed some insight into his expectations and ideal situation then we could have avoided such a terrible situation.

I had prepared as best I could for the meeting, I'd given thought to what was in the best interest of the children, taken my notes, done my breathing exercises, and was as ready as I'd ever be.

The family consultant was calm and polite, she seemed attentive to the children and was gentle in her communication with them; though they hardly spoke, they did play quietly together showing no signs of distress.

When it came my turn to speak with her one-on-one, I was honest, authentic and open, as well as organised and prepared. I spoke kindly of my ex, and even though he had made some serious accusations I shared my perspective of his personal challenges and the impact on our relationship, the children and the potential future.

If you find yourself in a similar situation, think about what you would like in the way of children's arrangements and why you feel it is best for your children from now until they're 18 years old.

Child Support

As most of us probably know, child support is financial assistance from one parent to another to assist in the costs of children in their care.[29] Consideration is given to:

- income of the parents
- time children spend with each parent

- the parents' ability to support themselves
- how many children
- other dependent children[30]

There are three ways to receive or make payments:

1. **Self-Management** – This is when you and your ex are amicable, and when there's no need to involve the child support agency (aka the Department of Human Services) or your employer(s). You agree between yourselves how much to pay or receive, and when and how you'll receive it. Ultimately, you manage the payments between you. Consider your family tax benefit here too (see the DHS website for more information).
2. **Private Collection** – Again, if you and your ex are quite amicable with each other this could be a good option. It's based on a child support assessment, one that you both agree, and has little interaction with the DHS, it's up to you to plan, manage and collect. Subsequently there are some options available if things get sticky and you need the DHS to step in and help.
3. **Child Support Collection** – For those that find it hard to communicate or get payment, this is the best option. Child support is calculated, and then money collected (where possible) from the paying parent and paid to the receiving parent. This is where I sit. My ex's child support has been in debt since it was first calculated over ten years ago. I only receive intermittent payments,

with no guarantee of when the next payment will come; that said with a child support collect option, there are ways they can collect overdue payments, such as deductions made by garnishing wages, or from tax return refunds.[31]

You and your ex have responsibility of the children until they're at least 18 years old, so now is the time to set some good foundations in place, for both you and for them.

6S ACTION points:

Visit www.helenslater.com.au to get your free:

- 6S Summary and Tips on what to include in a Parenting Plan
- 6S Transactional Analysis summary

Website links:

- www5.austlii.edu.au/au/legis/cth/consol_act/fla1975114/s60cc.html
- www.ag.gov.au/Publications/Pages/Parenting-orders-what-you-need-to-know.aspx
- www.familycourt.gov.au/wps/wcm/connect/fcoaweb/

family-law-matters/parenting/children-and-separation/children-and-separation
- www.familyrelationships.gov.au/sites/default/files/documents/06_2017/parenting-plans.pdf
- www.beanstalkmums.com.au
- www.servicesaustralia.gov.au/individuals/services/child-support/child-support-assessment/how-manage-your-assessment/compare-your-child-support-collection-options

Recommended reading:

- The Barefoot Investor, Scott Pape
- The Barefoot Investor for Families, Scott Pape

4

LEGAL PROCESS AND COURT PROCEEDINGS

Excuse Me Your Honour…

- Paperwork and Process
- Divorce
- Consent Order
- The Commonwealth Courts Portal - eFiling
- Initiating Application
- Section 60I Certificate
- Property Settlement Financial Statement
- Disclosure Documents
- Affidavit
- Notice of Risk
- Service of documents
- Response
- Application in a Case

- Contravention Order
- Applicant versus Respondent
- Court Attendance:
- What to expect
- Mention
- Hearing
- Trial
- Etiquette
- People Involved
- Court Orders
- Preparing to embrace change

There's a huge amount of paperwork involved in the legal process, whether you're involved in court proceedings or not.

Here's my quick recap of the three main aspects of family law:

1. Children Arrangements
2. Property Settlement
3. Divorce

In my case I commenced children arrangements and property settlement prior to divorce.

As mentioned previously, there's a deadline for property settlement after divorce; you must have at least commenced property settlement 12 months after your divorce is final.[1] That's not to say you have to have had sorted everything and agreed. It just means you must have started the court process, miss that deadline, and you'll be in a position where you'll need to ask the court for permission to make orders, and that isn't always granted.

If you don't finalise your property settlement formally or seek a divorce, from what I've encountered, there's no time limit on parties seeking another property settlement, in other words a couple who do not get divorced and finalise their property settlement formally leave themselves open for one of them to make a claim against the other.

It's not unheard of that a former spouse gets a second property settlement years after their separation if they didn't do it properly in the first place. And do you really want your ex turning up years later wanting to get their hands on the property you worked and saved for? I think not!

Divorce

In my experience the divorce application was the simplest as it turned out to be more of a paperwork exercise compared to children arrangements and property settlement; that said, there's a certain process and structure that is followed.

There are two options to apply for divorce. You can either apply solely or jointly.[2] Obviously, a joint application requires both of you to agree to the divorce and is a simpler process, compared to a sole application which requires extra steps, as outlined below.

Here's the basics outlined in my usual six-step summary format:[3]

1. Separate (you can still be living under the same roof though will need to provide evidence as to your separation).

And after 12 months and 1 day;

2. Complete and file/lodge your Divorce Application with the court via the Commonwealth Courts Portal. If it is a joint application, you both need to sign it before filing. If it is a sole application, only you need to sign it before filing.

Then with a minimum of 28 days before the divorce hearing date;

3. Serve (aka provide) your ex with a copy of your Divorce Application (if it is a joint application you won't need to do this).

Clarify whether or not you need to attend (see points below on sole and joint applications);

4. Have your divorce hearing.

If granted, 1 month and 1 day later;

5. Your divorce is final.

Celebrate your new life chapter;

6. Get your Divorce Order (available from The Commonwealth Courts Portal. Divorce Orders are no longer sent in the mail, you'll need to download it directly from the portal).

Depending on if you've made a joint or sole application to the court and whether you have children under 18 will affect whether or not you need to attend the divorce hearing.

- No children – you're not required to attend the divorce hearing
- Sole application – not required to attend
- Joint application – not required to attend
- Children under 18 and Joint application – not required to attend divorce hearing
- Children under 18 and Sole application – only the Sole applicant is required to attend, either in person or by phone on application[4]

If a respondent has filed a 'Response to Divorce' and does not oppose the application, they do not need to attend the hearing though they can if they want, and even if there is no 'Response to Divorce' the respondent can attend if they want, however, it is not necessary.[5]

Conversely, if a respondent has filed a 'Response to Divorce' and is opposing the application, then the respondent is required to attend the hearing as well as the Sole applicant.[6]

The only time the court will listen to a respondent opposing a divorce is when there is a claim that the separation date was less than 12 months before the date of filing.[7] If the court believes that the separation date was wrong, they will still allow the divorce, but it will delay the hearing until the 12 months are up.[8] So, the worst thing that can happen if/when the other party files a Response to the Divorce is that it will delay the divorce date.

Consent Orders

Consent Orders are when you and your former partner agree on the what, when, where, how and who.[9] Once you've agreed to 'terms' you can either type them up yourself/yourselves or you can get someone else to do it for you, whether that's your lawyer, your ex's lawyer or even other experts like separation & divorce accountants and coaches.

The necessary document to complete is a Form 11; Application for Consent Orders, which can be obtained from either a court registry or you can download a kit from the Federal Court of Australia website.

If you and your ex can agree and get Consent Orders in place you do not need to commence court proceedings. If, however, after meetings, mediations, and other genuine attempts, you're still unable and/or unwilling to agree on 'terms' and have no Parenting Plan or Consent Orders in place, then it's likely you'll need to commence legal proceedings to seek the court's assistance to make orders after hearing both sides (which is an expensive exercise).

Sometimes, parties settle 'on the court steps', which usually involves significant compromises for both parties; if there is no agreement, judges and other court officers can provide their opinions on how they would decide if there was a hearing.

In my experience, if you have a competent lawyer, they will know what's best for you and the children and they will be seeking this for you. I suggest that you listen to them, they know the law, they know what you're entitled to and how to work the law rules in your favour. Make sure you have a good relationship with your lawyer, it's essential that you not only give them clarity on what you want, but also hear what they have to say.

Some women I know think they're not worthy or aren't entitled to much as they were 'stay at home mums' or were predominantly home makers supporting their now ex through their career aspirations. This expectation, though common, is not how the legal process works.

The Commonwealth Courts Portal

The Commonwealth Courts Portal or 'the Portal', as it is affectionately known, is a virtual place where users file their documents and paperwork, and have access to information on their matter.[10] For example, what each party has filed, contact details (of course, there are exceptions where domestic violence is involved), law firm representation, court dates, judgments, Orders and so on.

To use the Portal to eFile you need to have the technology to do so, be able to make payments with a credit or debit card (aka VISA or MasterCard) and have access to a printer and/or scanner.

First step is to sign-up for access, just like you would with any other online resource, and from there you'll have access to the Portal to upload, download, view and make payment; think of it as an electronic filing cabinet, with all your necessary paperwork and related information.

Initiating Application

If you commence legal proceedings, you will need to complete an Initiating Application. This is the document you submit to the court to get your matter moving, and details what you want.[11]

Just like you apply for a passport or driving licence, you complete the necessary application form and then send it off to the appropriate place, there's also a filing fee. In your Initiating Application you will be able to detail 'Orders Sought'; this simply means what you are seeking in the way of final orders.

Should you decide to make an application to the court to start legal proceedings in relation to children's arrangements you will need to attach a document called a Section 60I Certificate to your application; this confirms that you attempted mediation (aka Family Dispute Resolution or FDR) prior to commencing legal proceedings.[12]

The court requires the Section 60I Certificate (or that you attend mediation), because some people will attend the mediation session(s) and come to an agreement on parenting arrangements and avoid going to court altogether.[13]

Section 60I Certificate

A Section 60I Certificate is confirmation that you and/or your ex attended mediation with a Family Dispute Resolution Practitioner (FDRP), or at least attempted mediation.[14]

For your Initiating Application to be successfully filed with the court, you will need to provide this certificate.

The Family Law Act requires that parents that are not in agreement about their parenting arrangements must initiate mediation and obtain a Certificate of Attendance (Section 60I Certificate) before an Application for a parenting Order can be made to the court. There are exceptions to this, for example, an urgent matter, domestic violence and/or child abuse. It's worth noting that you cannot compel the other parent to attend mediation, as it's an entirely voluntary process. You have to at least initiate the process, so that you can obtain the certificate, stating you tried to get the other party there.

Section 60I Certificates are issued whether you reach agreement or not, and whether you, or your ex, attend or not. The wording on the certificate varies depending on the outcome; some outline whether or not the parties made a genuine effort, whether one turned up and the other didn't, or whether the practitioner decided not to progress.

There are five types of Section 60I Certificates that can be issued in relation to Family Dispute Resolution (if it were me, there'd be six, to align with my personal philosophy and consistent six step processes, just saying!).

The five types of Section 60I Certificates are:

1. [name/s] did not attend FDR due to the **refusal or failure** of the other person or people to attend;
2. [name/s] did not attend FDR because the **practitioner did not consider it** would be **appropriate** to conduct FDR;
3. [name/s] attended FDR, conducted by the practitioner, and all people made a **genuine effort** to resolve the issue or issues in dispute;
4. [name/s] attended FDR, conducted by the practitioner, but one or more of them **did not make a genuine effort** to resolve the issue or issues in dispute;
5. [name/s] began FDR, but **part way through the practitioner decided** it was **not appropriate** to continue.[15]

If you feel dissatisfied with the Section 60I Certificate you receive, you have the option to attend mediation with a different FDR practitioner.

Using what you know about yourself and what you know about your partner, (see behavioural styles outlined in chapter one), will help you decide upon a realistic outcome, one that all those involved are in agreement with, now when I say agreement, this can sometimes be a compromise rather than an ideal collaboration. In my opinion if everyone's a little disappointed with the result, that's a good result. Which takes me nicely onto a conflict resolution framework/model.

Conflict Resolution model

Looking at the following conflict resolution model, you'll see the balance between assertiveness and cooperation. In an ideal world where collaboration is the best outcome, yet with tensions running high and conflict commonplace in legal disputes, compromise is sometimes considered a good result.

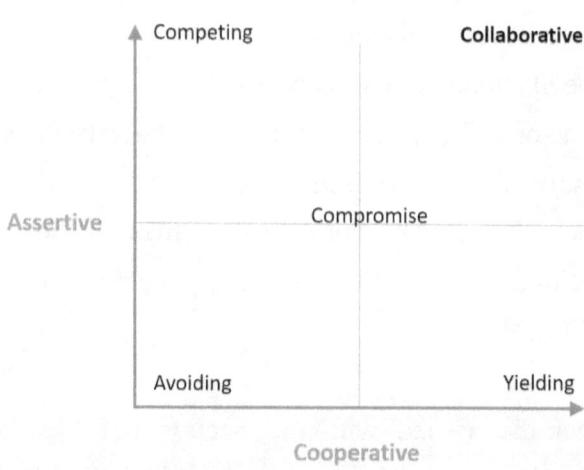

So, bear in mind that a compromise is not a fail or 'giving-in', it's more about showing willing and wanting a resolution to the situation.

Property Settlement Financial Statement

In relation to property matters, there is no compulsory attendance for mediating prior to filing an initiating application, not yet at least, though this is currently under consideration.

However, there is an obligation of disclosure, this means providing the other side with all information and documentation in relation to assets and liabilities you have.

You'll need to provide a completed Financial Statement which is around twelve pages long and outlines (six aspects, yep, there's my magic number again), your:

1. Income
2. Expenditure
3. Property/Assets
4. Superannuation
5. Liabilities
6. Financial Resources[16]

Additionally, if you're seeking some maintenance for yourself, the other party or your children, or child support, or financial enforcement, this should be detailed in form N (the second to last page of the Financial Statement document!).[17]

Disclosure Documents

Here's what I have found should be provided to the other side and what they in turn should provide to you:

- bank account details (account number and balance)
- bank account statements of each account from the past 12 months
- tax returns from the last three years
- payslips
- recent superannuation statements
- any Centrelink/pension/other statements
- shares and investments
- trusts
- life insurance
- partnerships and business information
- mortgage statements
- lease agreements
- credit card statements
- eBay account
- Paypal account
- loyalty programs (for example flybuys or frequent flyer points)
- loans
- evidence of any disposal of 'property/assets' in 12 months prior to, or since separation

Also include:

- valuations on vehicles (redbook valuations will usually suffice, at least for a start)
- other assets (like a boat, jet-ski, bike, trailer or caravan)
- household contents

- jewellery, antiques and collectables

Ultimately, you'll be providing a list of assets and liabilities (remember the Property Settlement chapter).

Affidavit

An affidavit is a sworn testimony of evidence,[18] in layman speak, it's a document that details information related to the facts of the situation, including things like:

- what happened (event)
- when it happened (date)
- people involved (who)
- the result (outcome)

It's a specific document with a specific layout (included in its format are headings, subheadings, numbered lines and spacing).

You can detail evidence and facts, whilst referring to certain specifics, for example, emails, texts, letters, photos, receipts, school report, as well as attaching them as annexures, also known as exhibits.

Recent changes have seen a limit on how many pages an affidavit, and its annexures can be, at the time of writing, for interim proceedings it was no more than ten pages for an affidavit and five annexures.[19]

You can find more information about completing affidavits in the court fact sheets, and via the court website.[20]

Interestingly, the only way my ex communicated what he wanted was in an affidavit, and a very nasty affidavit at that. It included accusations of child abuse and other ridiculous allegations. Still to this day I suspect that his solicitor at the time wrote the majority of his affidavit, as I would be truly sick if it was purely his words. One of the reasons I say this is that my original solicitor extracted information from me then drafted an affidavit for me to sign, and I was horrified to read the content, so much so I told them to re-write it and take out the nasty undertones. I wanted it to be factual, though I didn't want it to be belligerent.

I eventually fired that solicitor and got a new one! Then when I ultimately self-represented, one Judge referred to my material as 'refreshing' and made a Final Order at an undefended hearing. I'd stayed true to the facts, not gotten emotional and presented my material honestly and authentically; it paid off.

Notice of Risk

If there are issues of risk and/or domestic violence, then these should be detailed in the Notice of Risk document.[21] This document is included with all applications that are lodged with the court. It's a way of identifying and raising awareness of any child abuse or domestic violence issues and may be brought to the attention of the Department of Child Safety with a sense of urgency.

If after all your negotiations and mediation efforts nothing has progressed and you're wanting to start legal proceedings, here, in my usual six-point summary style, is what to prepare, complete and lodge:

1. Initiating Application
2. Section 60i Certificate
3. Financial Statement
4. Affidavit
5. Notice of Risk
6. Payment

When you file your initiating documents on the Portal, you should be able to select your own court date from the court's calendar, you'll then receive a sealed copy immediately. When you get this, you need to serve the other party so that they are aware of the impending proceedings and the court date, it also gives them an opportunity to respond.[22]

Service of Documents

Once you've filed your paperwork you need to serve the other party with it all, this includes the court's current designated brochures.[23] The most common way to 'serve' your ex is by handing the documents to them personally. That said, if you're sure the other party will sign an acknowledgement of receiving the documents, then they can be served by email or post.

You, as a party to the proceedings cannot serve the other party.[24] You can ask a friend or family member to serve your ex/partner and they will have to complete and swear an affidavit of service detailing how they served documents to the other party. If you engage a professional process server they will prepare this affidavit for you as this is usually part of their fee.

The affidavit of service should be filed with the court before the next court hearing so that you can prove you have served the other side. This is particularly important if your ex fails to show up as you'll be able to ask the court to make orders in your ex's absence on an interim basis.

Response

This is self-explanatory, the Response is the other party's response to a family law application (such as an Initiating Application or Application in a Case).[25] It includes completing the Response form as well as an Affidavit, Financial Statement and Notice of Risk.

The Response should be filed and served on the other party at least seven days before the Family Court court date[26] or within 28 days in the Federal Circuit Court, (the court date can be found on the first page of the Application).[27]

Application in a Case

Once matters are underway (known in legal speak as 'on-foot'), if there are any additional issues to address, another application can be made in the form of an Application in a Case.[28] In my case an example of this was to address the issuing of passports and travelling overseas.

Contravention Order

Contravention Orders can relate to:

- children arrangements
- non-children matters (such as sale of assets)
- a recovery order (preventing or hindering action under the recovery order)

If you, or your ex, breach any orders without a 'reasonable excuse', a Contravention Order can be brought before the court seeking some form of penalty or consequence.[29]

Some examples of the type of penalties are:

- Variation to any existing Orders
- Compensation for time lost with the child/ren
- Payment of most, or some of, the legal costs incurred by the other parties
- Compensation for reasonable expenses lost as a result of the contravention, e.g. travel costs, accommodation costs, etc.

- Participation in community service
- Fines
- Imprisonment[30]

A Contravention Order application cannot be filed via the ComCourts Portal, it needs to be filed at the court, either by sending hard copies in the post or visiting the Registry in person and taking hard copies with you.[31]

There is no specific response to a Contravention Order, however, the respondent can file a generic Response or an application seeking a variation to the existing order that the contravention relates to.

As mentioned previously there are some applications and documents you cannot apply for via the Portal, namely:

- Application for a decree of nullity/validity of a marriage
- Contravention
- Contempt
- Enforcements
- Reviews of a decision (appeals)
- Arbitration
- Third party debt notices
- Notices to intervene by a Third party
- Requests to issue a Subpoena

For these, you'll either need to send hard copies in the post or file by hand/in person at the court Registry (in some circumstances you may need to file via email).

Applicant versus Respondent

If you initiate legal proceedings, you are known as the Applicant and your ex will be known as the Respondent, also referred to as the Other Side (this encompasses your ex and his/her legal representation).

Quick clarification on this:

The Applicant is the person who completed and filed the Initiating Application; this is the paperwork to commence legal proceedings.

The Respondent is the person responding to the Applicant's application and paperwork.

It doesn't matter if you are the Applicant or Respondent in legal proceedings, there is no bias.

There is however a time limit on getting things started, this is called 'Statute of Limitation'.[32]

The current Statute of Limitation to initiate legal proceedings for a:

- Married couple is **12 months** after a divorce order becomes final.

- De facto relationship is **two years** after separation[33]

NB: A de facto relationship is defined as living together for two years or more.[34]

I commenced property settlement and children's arrangements before I applied for divorce. Most lawyers would recommend finalising property settlement before applying for divorce. Or at the very least to have filed an application for property division before filing for divorce. Doing it this way reducing the risk of you accidentally missing the time limit deadline.

Court Attendance

Going to court is an anxious time. I always suggest that my clients go to the courthouse prior to their first attendance and get familiar with the surroundings and the process. Everything from the layout of the building, to the security checks (it can be a bit like going through airport security). Go inside and see the courtroom and get a feel of the layout.

Knowing where you'll find your lawyer, as well as knowing where the toilets are, is a good way to reduce some of your anxiety and stress. Also, as it's usually an open court, this means you can go into the courtroom whilst a matter is being heard by the Judge and observe how things are conducted: who sits where, how the Judge interacts with the lawyers, what the clients do and don't do.

Typically on your first day of court, turn up, meet with your lawyer, (there may be some 'to-ing and fro-ing' between your lawyer and the other side), then when called you'll sit next to them in the courtroom and let them do the talking; they'll provide the Judge with details of your matter and what's happening and not happening!

Then the first 'return date' is an administrative hearing where the court wants to find out where each of the parties are and what progress has been made, if there's been any kind of agreement, or if most issues are in contention. Additionally, if one party has applied for interim orders these will be determined on this day.

Until you actually attend court, anything I say will just be helping to set basic expectations. If you have a court attendance coming up, go onto the Federal Circuit Court website to find out the dates of the family law 'sittings' (sitting just refers to the dates when family law matters are being heard) and go on one of those days and observe to get a sense of what you'll be in for.

Where I filed my application and documents we only had one family law sitting a month (whereas in the capital cities they have family law hearings every day). Attending my family law proceedings was very chaotic, with up to a few hundred people squeezed into a single floor level and with only one courtroom being used, tensions run high. Be prepared for delays too.

You'll be asked to be at court for 9am though it's extremely unlikely you will be seen at this time. When your matter gets heard by the Judge will depend on a few things. It's not an alphabetical process. The process of who gets to go first and so on is called a 'call-over', this is when all the lawyers meet with the Judge in the courtroom (without the clients) and agree what the next steps are with regard to being 'heard' and how much time it's likely to take, for example, if an interim agreement has been reached, or if there is a need to go to trial (this is called trial directions). As a self-represented applicant, I had to attend this meeting alongside all the other lawyers, including my ex's lawyer; and that was interesting to say the least.

If you've reached an agreement, interim or final, your matter will usually get heard early on as it's just a matter of sharing with the Judge that both parties are in agreement with the next step of getting the 'sign-off'.

If you have a lawyer you will also get heard before anyone who is self-representing as a self-representing litigant does not have to cover the hourly costs of a lawyer, whereas those who are paying for the lawyers' time to be at court with them will be given priority. I agree with this whole-heartedly. Unfortunately, this meant my matter was a long way down the list as not only was I a self-represented applicant I had no agreement from my ex on anything! Though him having his own lawyer worked in my favour as it meant he had more priority on the list placement and order of appearance, which by default meant I was seen earlier than if we had both been self-represented.

For ease of understanding, a typical order of appearance at court is as follows, remember, this is not always the exact order, and is my interpretation only, but it'll give you a base understanding and expectation.

1. Mention: The first time you appear in court, (in my case it was literally my name mentioned) where your lawyer will seek the court's assistance to help progress your matter. Usually the result is a court date for you to have a hearing. A mention is also a short hearing to update the Judge on progress.
2. Hearing/Interim Hearing: This is when evidence is presented to the Judge for consideration and decisions are made as a result. You can have many hearings, some may be to seek disclosure, some may be to agree on interim orders, or to progress with a family report. There are many potential outcomes. An important point to note: you can finalise proceedings by agreeing to Final Orders, then there's no need to go to trial. If there's no agreement, then you'll be seeking trial directions.
3. Trial: If after all your hearings your matter is still not progressing, it goes to trial. Trials are extremely expensive, time consuming and emotionally draining. It's not like it is in the movies AT ALL! There are many people involved in a trial and a significant amount of preparation is needed. This is when you'll enlist the services of a barrister too. It is a lengthy, expensive process.

Etiquette in the courtroom

The courtroom is a formal setting, and in my opinion if you want to give the best impression you should adhere to the rules of the court.

Also, some common sense is needed here! As much as you may want to give the other side 'f-you vibes' and make no secret of it, best to hold back.

Way back in the early 90s when I was training and coaching in the corporate world, I encountered a particularly good framework related to how we, as humans, make meaning and/or judgments of others, whether consciously or subconsciously. It was devised by Dr. Albert Mehrabian. His formula described how the mind determines meaning. He concluded that the interpretation of a message is **7%** verbal, **38%** vocal and **55%** visual, which means that **93%** of communication is "nonverbal" in nature.[35] Though this is still a debatable theory, it resonates with me and seems to have an important part to play in human interaction.

One of my favourite quotes from Ralph Waldo Emerson is: 'What you do speaks so loudly, I cannot hear what you say.'[36]

To summarise that:

- 7% is what you say
- 38% is how you say it
- 55% is how you look

Why am I mentioning this? Well, let's think about all the people who may become involved in your situation, from lawyers and Judges, to a family consultant, and members of society like teachers, the police, family and friends.

In the context of legal proceedings, if you do decide to enter the courtroom wearing inappropriate clothing, have an excessive amount of tattoos showing, or an overdose of piercings, be mindful that the Judge will have already formed some kind of opinion about you (subconsciously, or quite deliberately), and as unique and expressive as you'd like to be, the courtroom isn't the place. A compromise on this will serve you best in this situation, seriously do you really want to risk compromising time with your children or adjustments to your property settlement just because you want to be 'uniquely you', to 'make a point', to 'take a stand' or to 'defy the process and system'?

I've seen all types of outfit choices, some of the more memorable (for all the wrong reasons) were ripped jeans and a tee shirt saying 'FUCK YOU', I heard of person wearing a tee-shirt stating 'I'll nod to give the impression I'm listening' and the most eye-raising one, 'Suck My Dick, You'll Like It'. Some had denigrating comments about women, some were just inappropriate brands like FCUK (French Connection United Kingdom). Thongs and singlets are also a no no; need I go on? I'm sure you get what I'm talking about. It's also been said that Judges are known to pretend not hear the lawyer of an inappropriately dressed party, including those who leave sunglasses on their head.

Additionally, give some thought to your accessories, if you're arguing that you're poor, have no money, need a bigger chunk of the property pool, make sure you're not 'dripping in gold', there's a time and a place, court ain't the place to flaunt whatever wealth you may have.

The best way to think of it is not to be distracting in any way; wear neutral colours, minimal make-up and jewellery. Use your common sense.

Whenever the Judge enters or leaves the courtroom, you should stand. You will usually know when this is about to happen as a representative of the court will say 'All Rise' or 'Please Stand'.

Another expectation is to bow your head when you enter and leave the courtroom.

Do not chew gum.

Remove your sunglasses from your face and head.

Remove hats and caps.

Speaking in court is another formality. It's common practice to stand when the Judge speaks to you, and when you speak to the Judge. Address them as 'Your Honour'. Best not to interrupt, though make sure you've been heard and ask the Judge to clarify anything that you're unclear about. There are new rules in place that support self-representing litigants and I found the Judges were very receptive to assisting me as a self-represented applicant, of course if you have the support of a solicitor then they will do the majority of the talking for you.

Here's a list of some people who may be involved in your legal proceedings (in the order you'd likely encounter them, rather than alphabetically) that I have compiled based on my experiences:

- Lawyer/Solicitor/Legal Practitioner/Other Side – Self-explanatory.
- Process Server – Someone who serves documents to the other party. It can be someone you know or someone whose job it is to serve the other party documents (you cannot do this yourself, and it cannot be a child of the relationship).
- Judge/Judicial Officer – a person who has been appointed to hear and decide cases.
- Family Dispute Resolution Practitioner (FDRP)/Mediator – someone who attempts to help people reach agreement on a subject of conflict particularly with regard to parenting disputes.
- Family Report Writer/Family consultant – a psychologist and/or social worker who specialises in child and family issue.
- Independent Children's Lawyer – known as an ICL, they represent what's in your child's best interest.
- Registrar – a court lawyer who has been delegated power to perform certain tasks; for example, grant divorces, sign consent orders and decide the next step in a case.
- Barrister – a specialist who will represent you/your

matter in court, they differ slightly to a solicitor, and are involved in trials not 'normal' court.

- Cost Assessor – there are two main types here, one is someone who regularly reviews your file for the solicitor working on your matter and provides feedback on the amount of time and content ultimately leading to the detail on what the solicitor will charge you. Another is involved in court proceedings particularly in regard to those seeking costs, that is, requesting the other party to pay costs incurred.
- McKenzie Friend – a support person who is not a qualified lawyer, who supports self-represented litigants. This can be a friend or family member (you'll need to seek the court's permission for your McKenzie Friend to sit with you at the bar table, do this immediately after introducing yourself in court). Your McKenzie Friend will need to be objective, organised, calm and sensible, a good note taker and able to provide appropriate emotional support.
- Arbitrator – an independent person appointed to settle a dispute, and make a binding decision with the prior consent of both parties.
- Valuer – someone who estimates the cost of something.
- Forensic Accountant – someone who investigates the financial situation of business interests.

Court Orders

Court orders can be interim orders or final orders.

An interim order, as the name suggests, is an 'in the meantime' order[37] that is a bit like a stepping stone to getting to the final order, it's a work in progress, after all, final orders can take some time to reach agreement (or be court ordered, court orders!)!

A final order is the gold at the end of the rainbow (well, we all know that there isn't any actual gold at the end of the rainbow, yet the idea of it is enough to put a smile on our face), and like pots of gold at the end of rainbows, final orders can put a smile on our face, if only to signify the end of court proceedings on some level.

Sometimes the final order you're seeking can evolve differently once progress is being made, for example, you might decide that something you thought wasn't going to work turns out to be a good option after all, or conversely, something you thought would be a no brainer identifies potential red flags and causes concerns for a rethink, each can impact your thoughts on the final outcome. Always be open minded and forward thinking, use your head, trust your gut, follow your heart and pay attention to your intuition too.

When seeking final orders on parenting bear in mind that children are typically your dependents until they turn 18 years, so final orders that state pick-up and drop up times, supervised visits, shared holidays, accompanying trips and so on will vary in relation to the children's age. After all I don't think a teenager really wants supervising visits between them and the other parent, or being accompanied on days out, trips to the beach or even overseas 'excursions'.

During one of my court attendances, when the Judge was giving the judgment verbally, there was reference to the children travelling overseas 'in the company of the mother' (me) on all overseas trips, I highlighted the fact that some of the school excursions these days are opportunities to travel overseas and I wouldn't want my children to miss out because of a clause in the final order. The Judge understood completely and amended the judgment saying that as *'today schools have pretty fancy trips which can be overseas, I do not see that the order should be limited and the mother should have to come back to the court'* and subsequently omitted the 'in the company of the mother' clause. My point here is twofold, one: think long-term, and two: a Judge will listen to what you have to say, and if it's relevant they'll take any necessary action to assist in the process. Don't be shy about speaking up, just remember to be respectful.

Depending on your situation, it may be a good idea to consider adding into your order something about revisiting orders as the children age, after all, toddler needs are different to those of pre-teens and teenagers. So, whether that's the option to mediate or to agree to address in some other format (such as via email or in person), having a back-up to help set new expectations and guidelines takes away the potential need to go back to court.

When thinking about your future, give some thought to what you would like your ideal to look like as well as the impending interim periods. Now that you're in a different situation under different circumstances, embrace change and know that you have the opportunity to design a life that's tailored specifically for you, by you, with the potential for you to live your best life! The key words here are **embrace change**.

To reiterate my 6S six-step process for any aspect of change:

1. Start – be proactive. Get off the starting line.
2. Share – be open and honest with yourself and others.
3. Simplify – get back to basics; your personal values, the things that you like, what you're passionate about, what interests you and what's a priority.
4. Strategy – clarify your big picture and what you want. Create a basic Action Plan.
5. Structure – focus on your strategy and plan of action, start with tasks and deadlines and add them into your Action Plan to make it more specific. Review as you go.
6. Sustain – Practice effective habits, repeat, repeat, repeat!

Knowing where you want to be is your main outcome here. Once you have an idea of what you'd like your life to look like, the best way to make it happen is to have a strategy in place.

I like to define strategy as a plan of action designed to achieve a long-term or overall aim.

Here's my 6S steps of: Why, What, How, When, Where and Who?

1. Why: what's the purpose?
2. What: what's the outcome you're seeking?
3. How: the structure you'll do it in, the actions you'll take; create an Action Plan.
4. When: date and time, start and finish, commencement and deadlines.
5. Where: where will it happen location wise? In person, online?
6. Who: who are the key players, who's in your team, who's in your support network.

Spend some time to get your thoughts together and make it a priority to start creating an Action Plan. Get disciplined in taking action, meeting your deadlines and proactively ticking off your tasks and before you know it, you'll be progressing your goals and celebrating the wins along the way.

I know this is easier said than done, so here's the very first blog I wrote on goal setting titled *'Do It Yourself: Goal Setting for Success in Six Easy Steps'* and it's still relevant today.

WHAT IS A GOAL?

Question: What is a goal?

Answer: Depends who you ask!

I'm not talking about 'referees' blowing their whistle and the score at a home/away game, I'm talking about life goals.

Life goals are desires of where you want to be and, when broken down, are the roadmap and compass to help you get there. Goals provide direction for your life and context for your decisions. Goals ensure that you stay focused on your plan and keep you on the right track.

(Oh, and be mindful not to misspell Gaol; that's a whole different definition!)

WHY DO I NEED LIFE GOALS?

Goals keep you focused on the right direction and are key motivators because they help you feel inspired, motivated and empowered to live your best life. Who doesn't want that?

Whether you're seeking clarity on your 'where to' from here, or you're feeling overwhelmed, stressed, confused, unmotivated and/or lacking direction, then goal setting will help you get back on track and on the right path.

WHY IS IT IMPORTANT TO HAVE LIFE GOALS?

Without goals, most people tend to drift through life without direction; getting caught up in short term tasks and outcomes like paying the bills, watching TV, going shopping, going through the daily motions and generally just surviving. How about exchanging surviving for thriving?!

Success rarely happens by chance: ***success happens by design.***

The process of goal setting can be an enlightening experience (not in Buddha terms but more so in lightbulb moments). Giving some quality thought (and feelings) to what your 'ideal' would look like is a good starting point to understanding where to focus your attention and energy, as well as your time and finances.

WHERE TO IDENTIFY GOALS?

Consider the following areas:

- personal and professional goals
- work goals
- career goals
- financial goals
- mental goals
- mindset goals
- physical goals
- social goals
- spiritual goals
- emotional goals
- health & well-being goals
- relationship goals
- family goals
- parenting goals

How Do I Start?

Step ONE: IDENTIFY YOUR PERSONAL VALUES

Identify your personal values, i.e. what's important to you. These are personal traits that resonate with who you are and how you think/feel/behave. Values are traits or qualities that are considered worthwhile; they represent your highest priorities and your deeply held beliefs. A person usually stays true to his/her values, therefore developing goals from the perspective of your values means you are more likely to stay on track.

A few examples of values are:

- honesty
- ambition
- individuality
- integrity
- responsibility
- respect
- freedom
- loyalty

Step TWO: CLARIFY YOUR GOALS

Clarify your goals, the short term and the long term, and align them with your values. When goals are in alignment with your values you're more likely to achieve them.

Goals define what, where, and who you want to be, by when. Goals should be specific, enabling you to develop strategies to achieve them.

Write them down and make them SMART. I've included the traditional SMART acronym as well as my own personal SMART preference:

S – Specific (or Significant)

M – Measurable (or Meaningful)

A – Attainable (or Action-Oriented)

R – Relevant (or Rewarding)

T – Time-bound (or Trackable)

Keep goals positive because we attract what we focus on (plus the brain doesn't recognise the word 'don't': 'Don't think about pink flying elephants'; bet you saw some pink Dumbos!).

I regularly speak with stressed mothers about their communication with their child(ren), helping them to reframe their words so that they focus on the positive and get the result they really want. Some examples:

'Don't run' reframed to, 'walk please'.
'Don't shout' changed to, 'quiet voices please'.
'Don't push your sister' changed to, 'be nice to your sister'.

Get the idea?

I digress, back to goal setting basics.

Another framework I like to use is John Whitmore's GROW model. I had the privilege of collaborating with John (and his business partner, David) way back in the early 90s, and I still use this model today. I like to relate this to planting seeds not weeds!

G – Goals (SMART ones)

R – Reality (what is your current situation)

O – Options/Opportunities (solutions and possibilities)

W – Will (what you're willing to do, how committed are you)[38]

Step THREE: CREATE AN ACTION PLAN

Break your goal down into smaller actions; what you'll do, by when. Having a written plan gives focus and clarity and helps to manifest goals (seriously, the law of attraction is real science)!

Incorporate daily and weekly tasks, have a 'To Do' list, or three! One advantage of a 'To Do' list is that a tick equals achievement, so much so that when I've done something that wasn't on my list, I add it and tick it (yes, I do), this gives me a sense of achievement (yes, it does), and apparently has a dopamine effect that makes you feel good (yes again)!

Step FOUR: REVIEW PROGRESS

Be accountable for your actions. Regularly check-in on where you're at and how you're progressing, this helps maintain momentum, as well as giving you a sense of achievement, and keeps you focused on the right direction.

Step FIVE: AMEND ACCORDINGLY

If something isn't working, change it, whether it's actions, deadlines or behaviour. No mistake is wasted, it's all about learning and experimenting with what works best for you. You can't learn from mistakes you've never made.

Step SIX: CELEBRATE SUCCESSES

Maintain the habits that got you where you wanted to be. Celebrate small milestones, it's not just about the big end goal.

When you explore what's important to you, what interests you, what you're passionate about and what has priority for you, you'll get an understanding of your true motivators.

Ask yourself questions like:

- What do I really want?
- Where do I want to be?
- Who's with me?
- Where do I work/live?
- What do I do?
- How do I help others?
- What financial rewards do I get?
- What's important to me?

Additionally consider:

- What would you do if you knew you wouldn't fail?
- What if money wasn't an issue?
- If you were at your best, what would you be doing right now?
- What would you do if you didn't care what people thought?
- What does your ideal day look and feel like?
- How will achieving your goal affect others?

When you get to understand who you really are, where you really want to be and then create a plan to get there, you're already on the path to success.

IN SUMMARY:

1. Identify your Values
2. Clarify your Goals
3. Create an Action Plan
4. Review your Progress
5. Amend Accordingly
6. Celebrate your Successes

Your goals are your foundation for success!

Are you prepared to put in the time to think about your ideal and make that ideal a reality? Some of us can do this easily, others may need some support, either way the process of goal setting and action taking is life changing.

Take some time, whether that's a quick 10 minutes waiting in the car, mindful reflection in the shower, focused attention at the start of the day or designated time at the end of the day, wherever and however you can, start small to go big.

Whether you do it by yourself or have the support of another or others, your new life, new job, new house, new mindset, new you, is ready and waiting for you to grab it.

So, there you have it, my first blog on goal setting, read and re-read and start to implement actions that will help you progress to where you want to be in your life, whether that's an immediate goal or a long term goal. When you focus with structure and discipline, you'll be amazed at what you can achieve, I was!

6S ACTION points:

Visit www.helenslater.com.au to get your free;

- 6S Action Plan template

5

LAWYERS, LEGAL ADVICE, LEGAL COSTS AND LEGAL WORDS

From hand-holding to butt-kicking!

- Not going to court versus going to court
- The lawyer's office and the courtroom
- The lawyer's role
- Choosing your lawyer
- Self-representing
- Support team
- Legal costs x 3
- Legal language

You don't necessarily need the help of a lawyer. There, I've said it! I know so many people who have been wanting me to write that down, or at the very least say it out loud, for quite some time now; people who feel validated for their choice of consciously making the decision not to use lawyers, or people who have fallen victim to circumstance or financial constraints, dictating it as an outcome rather than a proactive personal choice.

For any lawyer that might be reading this, I am not anti-lawyers, far from it (if you've read the first half of the book, you'll know that). If, however, you've jumped straight into this chapter on lawyers and their role, then as you read on you might have raised eyebrows, a furrowed brow, or a general gnarly look about you (hey, don't shoot the messenger!).

Some lawyers were a little apprehensive about me writing this book due to the difference between legal advice verses legal information. I've made it very clear throughout this book that what I'm sharing is legal information and not specific legal advice. It's my own experience along with coping strategies to help those who are going through a separation so that they can be more prepared. What I am saying is that people should be seeking their own legal advice specific to their situation.

My role is primarily focused on helping people get their current situation into perspective, their future plan in place and to communicate effectively with their ex. I also provide support to rein in emotions, regain self-esteem, and introduce strategies to help rebuild their lives.

So, to you, the reader who's going through a separation, let me reiterate my aim for you:

1. Get your current situation into perspective.
2. Get your future plans in place.
3. Communicate effectively with your ex.
4. Rein in your emotions.
5. Regain your self-esteem and confidence.
6. Rebuild your life.

I regularly hold my clients' hands, metaphorically speaking. Though on a couple of occasions I have literally held their hands as they squeezed tighter and tighter, using me as their personal stress ball. This usually takes place in the lawyer's office or in a courtroom setting, yet it can also be via online support or part of their preparation prior to any potentially stressful interaction.

So, without further ado, let's talk about the lawyer's office and the courtroom.

If you are amicable with your ex then it's highly advantageous to stay out of the courtroom. I repeat, highly advantageous to stay out of the courtroom! Surely you know this, right? It's also worth noting that involving lawyers will immediately send a message to your ex that you're serious about progressing things. It may also be perceived as a sign of belligerence, whether intentional or not.

Before you engage a lawyer, let's briefly explore the options available to you, and a word to the wise, it's best to get consent orders or a financial agreement on property settlement before you finalise your divorce as this will stop your ex coming back for more later on, whether that's in a few months' time or years from now.

So, with regard to finalising your property settlement there are generally a few options, here are my, wait for it... six!

1. The DIY option

Do it yourselves using the resources from the Federal Circuit Court of Australia website and the Family Court of Australia, as that's where you'll find information on Consent Orders. Head on over to the website and have a look around at what resources are available. There's a specific section for 'the public' and 'Family law' with various sub-topics. You'll also see a 'Live Chat' tab where you can access direct guidance from a real human. Though they cannot provide legal advice, I found them to be very helpful in providing clarity on the process.

2. Speak with specialist accountants or financial advisors

Talk with a savvy financial advisor or accountant who specialises in property settlement for separating couples. They can help with the financials, including any superannuation splitting, and the best ones can draft your consent orders and lodge them with the court. This service will cost you, yet it's nowhere near as much as the cost of engaging a lawyer or costs associated with the ongoing process of legal proceedings.

Doing it yourselves or talking with a specialist accountant is a great option if you're amicable with your ex and you are both transparent about assets and liabilities. If, however, you are unable to communicate effectively together then you might want to consider the following options.

3. Family Dispute Resolution & Mediation

Attend a mediation session with a Family Dispute Resolution Practitioner (FDRP), aka a mediator, and agree what you can. You may be able to reach an agreement on property settlement (and children's arrangements).

Mediations can be:

- face to face in the same room together
- a shuttle mediation, where you'll be in one room and your ex in another
- by telephone either together or via a shuttle mediation
- via video conferencing like Skype or Zoom

There are government funded and subsidised mediation services throughout Australia through organisations like Family Relationships and Relationships Australia. These two organisations, though similar name, are in fact separate organisations.

Alternatively, you can pay for a private mediation. You might consider this option if your matter is urgent, has high conflict, or has a significant asset pool consisting of lots of companies and businesses, trusts and perhaps self-managed superannuation funds.

Private mediations usually cost around $5000 for a six-hour day, more on fees a little later in the chapter.

4. With lawyers – without going to court

Negotiation between lawyers. Engage the services of a lawyer and get them to assist with the asset allocation, aka property settlement, review or write your consent orders, file them with the court and get them stamped and returned. Or you could have a 'mix and match' approach: do some of the aforementioned yourselves, and have the lawyers do the rest.

Another option to consider is a Binding Financial Agreement (BFA), which is a written agreement between you and your ex, facilitated by your lawyers (you have your lawyer, your ex has theirs). You agree and finalise your property settlement in writing, signed by both you and your ex only after you have both received independent legal advice, which includes the effects of the agreement on your rights and the advantages and disadvantages at the time you sign. It must also be signed by each party's lawyer. BFA's do not need to be filed with the court.

5. Arbitration

Similar to mediation, arbitration is facilitated by an arbitrator who is a specifically trained and qualified legal practitioner who will, for want of a better description, behave like a Judge and have the power of a Judge.

Arbitration is like your own personal court hearing and you get to choose, when, where and with whom. It's a bit like a fast-track version of a trial yet less expensive, quicker and less formal. The arbitrator's decision is binding, it will be in writing, it'll detail the reasons for the decision and also include any facts and evidence that supports the final decision.

If a collaborative approach[1] (that is when parties work together to settle disputes and agree to stay out of court) or doing it yourselves is not an option, whether due to communication challenges, avoidance, domestic violence, or some other hindering issue, then you may need to seek the court's assistance and file an Initiating Application to get your matter before the court. You can do this yourself as a self-representing litigant or you can engage a lawyer to do it for you.

6. With lawyers – going to court

When you first meet with your lawyer, their suggestion will mostly likely be to try and agree to something without going to court, if they don't and have a 'gung-ho' approach to get you into court as soon as possible, consider why!

My top six pros and cons of lawyers' involvement:

Pros

- know the law
- may know your ex's lawyer too

- takes the pressure off you
- good middle person
- will help set realistic expectations
- does all the work

Cons

- expensive
- everything costs
- most of the control is with them
- your matter is not their only one
- time delays due to their availability, or lack thereof
- if you engage a lawyer first, it can be perceived by your ex as belligerent, that said, be empowered to be proactive

A crucial point to note is that if you end up in court proceedings, you'll need to agree to something to get out of the court system. You cannot simply ignore court dates as orders can be made in your absence (as was the case when my ex didn't attend court). Even if you and your ex agree, orders still need to be made, as an agreement made out of court is not legally binding.

Your Lawyer's Role

Lawyers should provide objective legal advice and guidance. They are there to get the best outcome for you, and discuss both the best-case and worst-case scenario.

Your lawyer wants the best for you, it's not just about money. This can be hard to believe at times particularly when they charge you for almost every interaction you have with them, from a phone call to a 'quick' email, to face-to-face meetings and court attendance, to reading the other side's emails and other documentation. Whatever the other side sends, it gets read and you get charged, whether it's relevant or not; this unfortunately is legal practice! More on lawyers' charges a little later in the chapter.

Choosing your lawyer

It's very important that you team-up with a lawyer that you're comfortable with, someone you feel you can trust, who you can be open and honest with. Your lawyer should align with, or at the very least, compliment your core values. Values are attributes that are important to you, from traits like integrity, honesty, trust, confidence and kindness, to qualities like freedom, independence, reputation and other aspects like family, health, and community.

There are literally hundreds of values, the ones you choose will be unique to you. Give some thought to your own core values, your ideals and that which you would like in your lawyer. Thinking back to the behavioural styles discussed in chapter one, you may identify yourself as an amiable person, being focused on people and feelings; great if you take on the role of counsellor, carer or healer, though consequently you may need a lawyer who possesses some traits that don't come easily to you, or are outside your core values. For example, you may need an analytical driver, meaning you may benefit from someone who is dominantly task or outcome orientated and interested in attention to detail. If you're a 'soft-soul' you may benefit from a lawyer with a 'bulldog' reputation who has a tough, tenacious and 'gets things done' approach.

I believe that most lawyers, by the very nature of the profession they've chosen, are inclined to be more dominant on the detail, facts, tasks and outcomes, they may have less interest in feelings; after all they are your lawyer, not your therapist.

Building good rapport is essential to any relationship or collaboration, from body language and words, to insight and intuition; and it's no different between you and your lawyer. Talk with your potential lawyer on the phone or in person and see how you feel about them. Do you get a sense that they 'get you', that they have 'what it takes' to communicate effectively with the other side and get a good result for you? Do they 'talk your language'?

Yes, lawyers are experts in their field of law, however, **there's more to family law and a separation than the legal aspect.** It's back to what we spoke about at the start; emotions and stress, mindset and self-management, relationships, communication, work, career, social and parenting.

It's a definite bonus if you can find a lawyer who views your matter from an holistic perspective, who not only identifies the specifics of your situation and circumstances but understands the bigger picture too, including those things that are affecting your day-to-day reality and your mindset, which in turn impacts all the other areas of your life.

A lawyer that has an awareness of your situation outside the legal aspects is a lawyer who can help prepare you not only for the legalities of a separation but also assist you with the successful transition to the next chapter of your life.

I know lawyers who refer clients to help with numerous things, like:

- getting into a positive mindset
- coping with stress and overwhelm
- enhancing relationships
- returning to the workforce, getting work ready
- managing their time
- getting organised

There are support networks available to you to help with every aspect of your relationship breakdown not only from the legal perspective, but all the other aspects too; emotional, mental, physical, financial, social, and spiritual. Find your supports and you'll be in a much better position going forward.

So many lawyers are only about the legalities and the money, without the complementary aspect of understanding you as a whole person: the stresses that you're going through, your emotional state, the challenges within your relationships whether with your ex, the children or other family members, the changing dynamics of friends and boundaries, work and colleagues: it's a very big arena that gets impacted. My best work has been with clients whose lawyers are happy to see their client with a support team rather than just seeing them as a legal client.

My suggestion to you would be to suss out how your lawyer feels about the big picture and the involvement and support of other people in your situation. Do they feel comfortable about you seeing other people, after all it's not like you're exclusively dating them! Ask if they refer their clients to other professionals who are outside their scope of practice (like counsellors and/or coaches) and see how they react. Their reaction will give you a good indication as to whether they are open to the possibility that someone else other than them can assist you during your separation. Or you may see them turn into a green-eyed monster (figuratively speaking) or even observe some narcissistic qualities come to light. Balance your head and instinct, listen to your gut and trust your intuition.

Whenever you're feeling stressed, overwhelmed or conflicted, the best thing to do is to be clear about what you want. Get clarity with your goals by beginning with the end in mind. Always ask yourself 'what's the outcome I want from this?'. Knowing your ultimate goal will assist you in your decision making and also help with any potential compromise; whether that's in choosing your lawyer or during any negotiations.

The First Appointment

Prepare properly for your first appointment so that you get the best legal advice, otherwise you're at risk of the meeting turning into a 'fact-finding' exercise or a therapy session where you just end up crying or venting your anger.

I know some good lawyers who are indeed very attentive to the emotional release of clients, but like they say, *'I'm not your therapist, you pay me the big bucks to sort out your legal matter so let's concentrate on that'* (cue the passing of the tissue box; every lawyer's office should have a decent supply of tissues, and wine, yes, wine too, for those late afternoon, early evening appointments or is that just me?).

Go to your first appointment ready with relevant information. Here's a quick list of some information to take and prepare for in advance:

- The usual personal details: full name, date of birth, contact details (have your driving licence, passport or other identification documents on hand as most law firms will want to take a copy of your driving licence or at least some form of identification).
- Significant dates: start of relationship, duration of relationship, wedding date, separation date, children's birthdays, and anything else you believe will be of use.
- Combined current assets and liabilities (a ballpark figure for each asset and debt is fine).
- Income and expenses (ballpark figures are fine).

- Children arrangements, age, schooling, health, any specific needs.
- Any issues of Domestic Violence.
- Any questions you may have.

If you take documentation with you, such as tax returns, superannuation statements, bank statements, information on shares and interests in companies and trust, this will assist your lawyer in understanding your matter better and will allow them to give you the most appropriate legal advice.

This is probably a good time to mention that the cost of your initial appointment and advice given in person is one element. If you decide to engage with that particular lawyer you will also be charged for the work that supersedes the appointment, that is the writing up of notes from the meeting, setting up your files (both electronic and hard copies), a summary of what was said, information and documentation received and advice given. Usually you'll receive some correspondence confirming what was said and discussed, along with a Client Agreement sometimes referred to as a Legal Services Agreement.

Fortunately, by the very nature of legal practice, lawyers are required to follow specific guidelines and adhere to strict regulations, both with regard to in-house processes and procedures as well as client interactions.

The first noticeable process is when you initially contact a lawyer. The first thing they'll ask is for your personal details and those of your ex as they'll need to do a 'conflict check' to find out whether your ex has already been in touch with them. If your ex has, unfortunately that becomes a conflict of interest and they will not be able to progress any further with you.[2] They will tell you straight away whether they can help you, or not.

Some lawyers provide a short free initial consultation either in person or over the telephone. Seldom has anyone I know been able to gain specific advice within such a timeslot. However, it's a great way to explore whether that firm or lawyer is a good fit for you.

If a private law firm is out of reach for you, or the timing isn't quite right yet, there are some fabulous lawyers who give their time voluntarily or provide their services within a charitable organisation, some of the best and most accessible will be at your local community legal centre. They rely on donations and government grants and provide a fantastic service so utilise their services where you can.

Think about what you can do yourself. Prep and Preparation!

You do not need a lawyer to do your property settlement, however, if you do engage a lawyer you can reduce some of your legal fees by doing some of the work yourself; consider becoming your own administrator. Why pay a lawyer's office to do admin tasks you can do yourself? If you're going through a property settlement you can make arrangements to obtain, collate, photocopy and organise your disclosure documents.

Self-representing

This is not for the faint hearted. Family law matters can be complicated and where possible I would certainly suggest the services of a lawyer. Lawyers know their stuff, they know the law, they know what to say, how to say it and what to ask.

Bear in mind with the help of a lawyer you may never go to court, all matters can be resolved outside of the courtroom. If you self-represent, you are likely to end up in the courtroom, in front of a Judge with a qualified lawyer on the other side. This is not the ideal scenario and whatever you thought you'd save on legal fees you'll probably end up spending (that and more) in court fees and legal expenses. And ultimately you may not get what you expected both in parenting and property.

Consider whether you'd be better off paying for the services of a lawyer and getting your best result, rather than going it alone and dealing with the maze of legal processes, procedures and paperwork, including your own personal blind spots and those insights needed to navigate the process. It can be a lonely road, doable, yet very time consuming, stressful, mentally challenging and emotionally draining. I speak from personal experience.

I just mentioned personal blind spots, these are aspects that are unknown to you and can hinder your progress. In the early 90s, I was introduced to a framework that was a lightbulb moment for me with regard to understanding my own self-awareness, or rather lack thereof, as well as facades and assumptions. It's called the Johari Window[3]. The Johari Window framework is predominately about improving your own self-awareness and understanding your relationship with yourself and with others.

The reason I have included the Johari Window framework is that it is a simple yet effective way to help give you some awareness of how you may see yourself, and also how others may see or know you too.

I've adapted the original framework to include an additional 6S aspect to help you not only have an awareness of the situation but to take action too.

It's important to be aware of what you can do yourself and where you may need support, from the practical to the emotional aspect.

Having an awareness of how you can effectively communicate with your lawyer and your ex is always going to be beneficial whether you self-represent or not.

Sometimes just having to deal with your ex can be a challenging task in itself and one that can hinder you at the very first step. At least with a lawyer on your side 'doing' the work and dealing directly with the other side, you don't need to get involved directly which can prove to be a bonus, this was particularly so in my case. Your lawyer becomes the 'filter' for any of the other side's nonsense. They'll also tell you like it is, helping to set realistic expectations. Ironically, it was a lengthy email from my ex to my lawyers that was the deciding factor on my decision to self-represent.

I believe self-representation is more commonplace now due to people not having the financial resources to utilise the services of a lawyer, and still not being eligible to have the assistance of legal aid.

Support Team

Whichever way you go, get your support team together; whether that compromises of your lawyer, a counsellor, your doctor, and close friends and family. Oh, a word of caution with friends and family, though they may be well-meaning and have good intentions, their bias and potential anger around the separation process may hinder your progress rather than help it. Plus your friends don't always want to hear about your relationship breakdown and separation, whether that's because it puts them in an uncomfortable position, or that it seems a continuous barrage of your woes!

Consider colleagues, like-minded friends and acquaintances, for example your yoga class, sports team, church group, and your neighbours too, though don't overdo it – you don't need to share everything with everybody.

Having the support of a good divorce coach or life coach can help you gain clarity and confidence to focus in the right areas, whilst also providing an holistic approach of support to all aspects of your life.

You may have heard the term 'McKenzie Friend' (if you've read chapter four you certainly would have). This is someone who is your legal support person and although not legally trained, they are able to assist you if you do not have legal representation. Something, and someone, to consider if you find yourself self-representing.

When I'm part of a client's team I get to wear many hats. Sometimes I provide empathy and hand holding, other times I provide accountability and butt-kicking. Eventually I'm a cheerleader supporting the client to embrace change and celebrate the wins, no matter how small.

LEGAL COSTS x 3

Let's talk about the elephant in the room: how much will all this cost? Unfortunately, there is no package price for going through a separation. However, there are specific costs in relation to specific aspects. Here's a quick distinction between Lawyers Charges, Court Fees and Legal Costs:

Lawyers Charges

These are your lawyer's fees. Your lawyer will charge you for their services which includes everything from their hourly rate for legal advice for in-person meetings, behind the scenes, and any advice over the phone and in emails, including costs for preparing documents, writing emails, perusing material like bank statements, superannuation paperwork, reading correspondence from the other side, and also taking any phone calls in relation to your matter.

Lawyers more often than not charge by the hour. Also they usually charge in six-minute increments outside of their hourly rates which is the equivalent of one tenth of an hour and when you consider a six-minute phone call can cost you around $35, best to be sure you really need to talk. So, let's say you call your lawyer and speak for just two minutes, you'll actually be charged for six minutes, if you call and speak for seven minutes, you'll be charged for twelve minutes, it's all rounded up!

Additionally, when it comes to reading a document you'll usually be charged per words; typically, 100 words (known as a folio) which can cost you between $10 to $50+ depending on the content and outcome, and this can be in addition to the lawyers hourly rate (a little bit of 'double-dipping' me thinks!).

My point here is it can be more cost effective to arrange a face to face meeting and have the lawyer read relevant content during the appointment, that way you'll be charged for the hourly rate only, no additional costs on reading words or rounding up minutes (well, some lawyers might round up the minutes, be mindful).

You'll be charged for:

All attendances, that is, any time that your lawyer spends working on your matter whether you're present or not. From meetings, conferences, telephone calls, court appearances, travel times, and wait times, to preparation of documents, including writing a debrief from any interaction; whether a detailed memo from an appointment or a file note from a phone call, it all gets written up, shared and filed.

Expenses paid on your behalf (these are the disbursements) from court filing fees and court event fees, to title searches and paying other people like process servers and family report writers. Cost assessors too, independent experts who assess the amount of work done on your file, including folios (remember the 100 words) and then assign that time, and those details, to your lawyer who in turn charges you, not only for the assessors' time but their recommendations too; wait, what's that now? Yep, you get to pay for the privilege of a cost assessor to review your file (well around 50% of the costs), now don't you feel enlightened!

Process servers cost; your lawyer will arrange this for you. Or if like me, source one yourself. Be prepared to provide all the relevant information, including a recent photo of your ex (or whomever is to be served) is helpful. I've heard of some process servers costs being as low as $50. Realistically though, I'd suggest a budget of around $80 to $150 for this service. You can ask a friend to serve the documents to your ex, though like anyone serving documents, they will still need to complete an affidavit to confirm the details of when they served the other party, how, when, where, what happened, and what was said. You cannot serve documents yourself.[4]

Copying also costs whether it's the old school photocopier, scanning documents via email or any other electronic transmission: text, messenger or fax, and these costs can certainly add up particularly when you consider a single photocopy can be charged to you at around $1. Quick observation, tell me, apart from lawyers who even has a fax these days?

To recap, here are the Lawyers Charges in my usual six-point summary:

1. Attendance – meetings, conferences, mediation, court, travel and wait times. (Attendance in person is one aspect, the write up of the notes, advice and actions taken afterwards are additional attendance, as the lawyer is 'attending to your matter'. It's not like a typical appointment, whereby you have your appointment, pay and leave, job done. No, you have your legal appointment, pay for that time, then incur additional charges as a result of the work that needs to be written up or actioned as a result. You pay for the lawyer's time in the room, and the lawyer's time outside the room.)
2. Telephone contact – with you and others relating to your matter.
3. Correspondence (letter, email, text, messenger or fax) – given and received.

4. Documents – preparation, reading, perusing and copying – given and received.
5. Expenses (disbursements) – paying other people and organisations.
6. Hourly rates – of the lawyers (commonly range from $360 to up to $650 per hour) and admin staff too. A legal assistant's time can be charged to you at up to $140 per hour and is certainly not reflected in their salary. Hmm, I feel that this is a cheeky charge!

And I've saved the best for last; I've not included it in my aforementioned six as it's certainly outside the box, so much so that I don't know of any other profession (if there is, please let me know!) that charges a 10% - 35% Care and Consideration fee. That said, not all lawyers charge this, so check your Legal Services Client Agreement. I consider this a 'top-up' fee and it really gets my goat, why? Because it's a charge over and above what you're already paying! I believe it's essentially a 'back-up' cost, charging you for the lawyer to 'get it right'! I know some lawyers reading this will be thinking 'that's not what it is', I can already hear them saying something along the lines of 'it's about the extra work that goes into a matter', to that I respond with: sounds like double-dipping to me! The actual words are 'care and consideration' which surely should be a given to any client matter, after all I think it's fair to say that a client would have the expectation that the lawyer is always providing care and consideration to their case. Seriously, imagine a surgeon charging an additional cost for 'care and consideration'! Okay, rant over.

Now, on the plus side lawyers should not be charging you for correspondence relating to your fees and accounts, some also agree not to charge for internal memos and emails between solicitors and team members as well as some other aspects too.

What is charged and not charged will be outlined in your Legal Services Client Agreement (this is a legal requirement of the Legal Profession Act[5]). Likely to be a lengthy document, it details the terms and conditions of the service provided to you by the law firm or lawyer as well as your individual rights and obligations. Your relevant state/territory Law Society will have a copy of 'Legal Costs – your right to know' on their website.

Read and re-read your Legal Services Client Agreement contract and terms and conditions and ask your lawyer for clarity if you have any questions. All costs and expectations will be outlined in that document. I know we don't all read the small print, yet on this occasion it will serve you well to know what you're going to be charged for and how much.

Court Fees

The court charges filing fees and court event fees. Filing fees are related to the filing of documents; just like you put in an application for a passport or driving licence, you complete a form and send it off with the payment, the same goes for any application you submit to the court.

Filing Fees are incurred for an:

- Application for Consent Orders
- Application for Divorce
- Initiating Application (differing combinations, for example, parenting and/or financial, final and/or interim)
- Response to Initiating Application
- Interim Order Application/Application in a Case
- Issue of Subpoena

Court Event Fees relate to when you are due to be in the courtroom, for example, when you attend court for a hearing or a conciliation conference. Think of it like hiring a room and the services of the people involved (Judge or Registrar), though not your lawyer, they will charge you their own fees.

Court Event Fees, 1) setting down for hearing fee, 2) daily hearing fee, 3) conciliation conference.

Separating and going through the legal process is expensive, so it's important to know what costs are involved.

When you engage the services of a lawyer, you'll be presented with their Legal Services Client Agreement to read, agree and sign, this sets out the terms and conditions of your interaction with your lawyer and additional aspects of your matter.

A quick word of warning: don't believe anyone who says it can all be settled within a $2,000 budget. This is what I was told by my very first lawyer, even though I explained to him that the relationship was not particularly amicable, that my ex withheld information and had control of all the finances, that young children were involved and that my ex was avoidant in all areas of communication – including disclosure and time, finances and children, past and present plans and future expectations.

As my ex's communication on both children arrangements and property settlement was non-existent, it was practically impossible to make any progress. I had attempted to discuss and agree both property and children arrangements without the involvement of lawyers, however, after seven months of trying to gain some headway, nothing progressed (in fact we were going backwards instead) and as a result my ex gave me no other option than to sign the dotted line for legal representation and engage the services of a lawyer. My first lawyer did not understand my matter and ultimately failed me. I fired them and got new representation.

Now, even though I am very budget orientated and like to keep an eye on my income and expenditure, I don't mind sharing with you that after spending $30,000 on legal costs, I lost count of the monies exchanged. What I do know is that it's not just about the financial cost, it's also the emotional and mental cost and you can't put a price on that.

To give you an idea of specific costs, head to my website for the link to the current court fees. The specifics covered are for filing fees and court event fees.

Unless you're self-representing, most of the people involved in your matter will be paid via your lawyer, who will in turn invoice you.

The most common practice is when your law firm holds an amount of between $2,000 to $5,000 in trust to cover the costs of your matter as you go along, replenishing the funds when they run low. Some lawyers may be prepared to take some of the money after your matter is concluded, though most use the trust account method.

I get a lot of clients complaining about the bills from their lawyers. What's important to remember is that lawyers not only charge you for their time, which is a higher end hourly rate to most, but they also bill you for court costs and other alliances like that of process servers, cost assessors, family report writers and others who may be involved in your matter. So, all in all the invoice will no doubt take your breath away!

If you are more informed and have a realistic expectation of your legal invoices, you will feel better about your lawyer's fees and any associated costs. Yes, they're renowned as one of the most expensive professional services so think about what you can, and cannot, do yourself and adapt where possible.

Be mindful of things like how sending five emails will attract more fees and subsequently a bigger invoice than waiting until the end of the day or week and incorporating all the points in one email.

There are benefits to having a lawyer on your side, one is that they may be able to get you a greater percentage of the asset pool so when you consider paying $30,000 in legal fees to get an additional $100,000+ from the asset pool, this is certainly a good investment, that's a $70,000 gain. That didn't happen for me unfortunately, but I do know of clients who have come away with a bigger chunk of the asset pool due to the savvy play of an on-point lawyer.

There are two courts to consider regarding Family Law fees; the Family Court of Australia and the Federal Circuit Court of Australia (formerly known as the Federal Magistrates Court of Australia). And if you live in WA, the Family Court of Western Australia.

Both courts deal with family law matters. The Federal Circuit Court of Australia deals with nearly 80% of all family law matters. The Family Court of Australia is a superior court that has specialist judges and staff to help resolve the most complex of legal family disputes, as well as consent order applications. Each court has its own fees.

If you hold certain Government concession cards or you can demonstrate financial hardship, you may be eligible for an exemption of fees. See the Guidelines for exemption of court fees at www.familycourt.gov.au and www.federalcircuit-court.gov.au.

Legal Language as taken from the Family Court

Abuse – in relation to a child, is defined in subsection 4(1) of the Act. For convenience, the definition is set out below with the definition of 'Family Violence'.

Address for service – the address given by a party where documents can be served on them by hand, post or some other form of electronic communication.

Adjourn – defer or postpone a court event to another day.

Affidavit – a written statement by a party or witness. It is the main way of presenting the facts of a case to the court. An affidavit must be signed before an authorised person (such as a lawyer or Justice of the Peace) by way of swearing on the Bible or attesting to the truth of the contents of the statement.

Appeal – a procedure which allows a party to challenge the decision made by a court.

Applicant – the person who applies to a court for orders.

Case – when a person makes an application to a court for orders, that becomes the case before the court.

Consent order – an agreement between the parties that is approved by the court and then becomes a court order.

Contravention – when a court finds a party has not complied with (followed) a court order, that party is in contravention of (or has breached) the order.

Court hearing – the date and time when a case is scheduled to come before the court.

Court order – the actions the parties or a party must do to carry out a decision made by a court. An order may be either interim or final.

Divorce order – an order made by a court that ends a marriage.

Enforcement order – an order made by a court to make a party or person comply with (follow) an order.

Ex parte hearing – a hearing where one party is not present and has not been given notice of the application before the court; usually reserved for urgent cases.

Exposed to family violence – is defined in section 4AB(3) of the Act. For convenience, the definition is set out below with the definition of 'Family Violence'.

Family consultant – a psychologist and/or social worker who specialises in child and family issues that may occur after separation and divorce.

Family dispute resolution – a process whereby a family dispute resolution practitioner assists people to resolve some or all of their disputes with each other following separation and/or divorce.

Family Law Act 1975 ('the Act') – the law in Australia which covers family law matters.

Family law registry – a public area at a Family Court and Federal Circuit Court where people can obtain information about the court and its processes and where parties file documents in relation to their case.

Family report – a written assessment of a family by a family consultant. A report is prepared to assist a court to make a decision in a case about children.

Family violence – means violent, threatening or other behaviour by a person that coerces or controls a member of the person's family (the *family member*), or causes the family member to be fearful. A child is exposed to family violence if the child sees or hears family violence or is otherwise exposed to family violence. See the Family Law Act, section 4AB, which gives examples. Family violence may also amount to child abuse.

Abuse – in relation to a child means,

a) an assault, including a sexual assault, of the child; or

b) a person (the *first person*) involving the child in a sexual activity with the first person or another person in which the child is used, directly or indirectly, as a sexual object by the first person or the other person, and where there is an unequal power in the relationship between the child and the first person; or

c) causing the child to suffer serious psychological harm, including (but not limited to) when that harm is caused by the child being subjected to, or exposed to, family violence; or

d) serious neglect of the child.

Family violence order – an order (including an interim order) made under a prescribed law of a State or Territory to protect a person from family violence.

Filing – the procedure of lodging a document at a family law registry for placing on the court file.

Final order – an order made by a court to bring a case to a close.

Form – a particular document that must be completed and filed at court. Different forms are used for different family law matters.

Independent children's lawyer – a lawyer appointed by the court to represent a child's interests in a case.

Interim order – an order made by a court until another order or a final order is made.

Judgment – a decision by a court after all the evidence is heard.

Judicial officer – a person who has been appointed to hear and decide cases; for instance, a judge.

Jurisdiction – the authority given to a court and its judicial officers to apply the law. For example, the courts have jurisdiction under the *Family Law Act 1975* in family law matters.

Parental responsibility – the responsibility of each parent to make decisions about the care, welfare and development of their children. These responsibilities may be varied by agreement or by a court order.

Parenting plan – a written agreement between the parties setting out parenting arrangements for children. It is not approved by or filed with a court.

Party or parties – a person or legal entity, such as a corporation, involved in a court case; for example, the applicant or respondent.

Precedent – a decision made by a judicial officer, which may serve as an example for other cases or orders.

Procedural order – an order made by a court of a practical nature. For example, the court may order the parties to attend family dispute resolution.

Registrar – a court lawyer who has been delegated power to perform certain tasks; for example, grant divorces, sign consent orders and decide the next step in a case.

Respondent – a person named as a party to a case. A respondent may or may not respond to the orders sought by the applicant.

Rules – a set of directions that outlines court procedures and guidelines. The rules of the Family Court are the *Family Law Rules 2004* and the rules of the Federal Circuit Court are the *Federal Circuit Court Rules 2001*.

Service – the process of sending or giving court documents to a party after they have been filed, in accordance with the rules of court. Service ensures that all parties have received the documents filed with a court.

Subpoena – a document issued by a court, at the request of a party, requiring a person to produce documents and/or give evidence to the court.

Transcript – a record of the spoken evidence in a court case. All court hearings are recorded, except uncontested divorce hearings. The court does not order transcripts in all instances and does not provide transcripts to parties. If a party orders a transcript, they will be responsible for the costs.

6S ACTION points:

Visit www.helenslater.com.au to get your free:

- List of what to take to your first appointment with a lawyer.

6
MY STORY

Past, Present and Future

From surviving to thriving, and thriving from here.

Well, if you've made it this far through the book, I hope you've gotten some separation insights into what to expect, what to consider, how to get organised, who can help you and how you can help yourself.

My purpose for sharing my story and personal insights is to help you be more informed, gain clarity and to give you a sense of expectation. As well as provide you with strategies to inspire you with confidence, so that you can make it through your separation in one piece.

My separation happened over ten years ago, yet I still deal with my disruptive ex. Unfortunately, my situation is not uncommon.

I hope that you can find some equilibrium and amicability in your relationship with your ex so that you avoid discord and disruption.

Ironically, whilst finalising this book, my ex, after a few years' hiatus, made a reappearance via Legal Aid. Even with final orders and a physical absence of nearly ten years, he continues to 'pop up' every two or three years or so, bringing disturbance and disruption with him.

From being inundated with verbally abusive emails and texts, to a quieter inbox after being granted a Protection Order (particularly with regard to stalking, emails and texts), the past four years have been calmer and more settled for both the children and me.

However, as I put my story to paper, I received an email from him. He asked me to 'forgive' his child support debt, and that if I didn't, he would, 'have the option to go to court' and, 'that would involve serving [me] papers for this process'. *Hmmm*, so here we are again. Do *this* or I'll do *that*, seems like nothing has changed. I decided to ignore his email, and low and behold I received correspondence from Legal Aid inviting me to mediation.

The mediation was conducted via telephone and via a shuttle service. The mediator spoke with each of us separately without the other hearing what was being said. They talked with my ex first, as he initiated the process, whilst I waited for the subsequent phone call to update me on the 'what' and 'why'.

Then when the mediator talked with me my ex waited for them to go back to him. It was a safe space for both of us to share perspectives, facts, expectations and agree on the next steps. I agreed to almost everything my ex asked for in the hopes of building some small and healthy reconnection between him and the children. The one thing I did not agree to was related to the children's school.

During mediation it was agreed that the children's school would continue to remain confidential. Yet, exactly one month to the day, I received a phone call from the children's school advising me that my ex had sent an email seeking information on the children. What ensued was me making some phone calls and having numerous conversations with the governing bodies of not only the school but also the Queensland Department of Education. From their feedback we believed my ex, now having some clue as to where I was living, had contacted all the schools in the local area, sending a blanket email to each school's administration in the hopes that someone would reply. It's an expected behavioural pattern of his. When he's told 'no' he takes it on himself to defy whomever and whatever.

Just as he was told 'no' in court proceedings, he defied them, to his detriment, as orders were made contrary to his actions and in his absence. He defied a temporary protection order which then lead to a final protection order being granted. He defied paying child support, still does, and now the government takes it directly from him. Okay, let's not dwell too much on the negatives and reframe it: it's good to know that there are consequences for detrimental actions.

You may have a similar experience with your ex whose behaviour may test your patience and your resolve. Ironically, it was my ex's behaviour that ultimately led me to self-represent.

Self-representing

There were certainly some highlights during my time self-representing, from gaining confidence and understanding the process, to receiving respect in the courtroom.

One highlight was when I was in the courtroom and I received a particularly complimentary comment from a Judge. He found my court material (my documents and evidence) *refreshing*! Now, I'm sure that doesn't sound like much to you, but if you knew the Judge and the context, you'd be suitably impressed, my hand-holding solicitor certainly was when I told her!

I've been before a handful of judges, not just one consistently through my matter and on this occasion, I was before a new one for the first time. I'd sat in the back of the courtroom observing his style which was direct to say the least. He seemed quite formidable and I'd been told he was renowned for giving lawyers a 'hard time'. To say I was anxious and a little nervous was an understatement. Though, as it turned out, I had nothing to fear. He was empathetic to my situation, he was perplexed at the lack of progress within the timeframe and he was ready to hear my case on a final basis, if I was ready to give it!

Having the opportunity to be heard, for the Judge to proactively facilitate the progress of my matter, and for it to be finalised gave me a renewed sense of confidence in the process and the outcome.

It's very common that at the end of a final hearing, a Judge does not make a final decision. They often 'reserve' their decision to a later date. This gives them an opportunity to consider the specific evidence of a case before deciding which orders would be best. It is not unheard of to have to wait a year or so before a decision is made.

During my 'final hearing' the Judge gave his 'reasons for judgment' of a final order – this is a verbal description of what, why and how it relates to the *Family Law Act* 1975.

I was fortunate enough to be one of the few who not only got a judgment quickly after a hearing, but immediately after.

There were many solicitors in the courtroom that day listening to the Judge's decision. I understand that it is quite unusual for solicitors who are not involved in a case to be interested in its outcomes. I'd like to think they were there because a self-represented litigant, me, was providing argument and this 'formidable' Judge had made a decision and was giving his reasons for judgment. That said, ultimately I cannot speculate why they were there.

As I left the courtroom that day, I was approached by a couple of solicitors who were aware that I was in the process of supporting others as a 'divorce coach'. They explained they were impressed with what just happened and we exchanged business cards. So began the 6S Coaching story.

Even though final orders were granted in early 2011 on both parenting and property, nearly two years later I was again before the court. This was due to my ex not agreeing to anything: not to time, not to child support, not to signing of passports, not to school enrolments, not to holidays, not to time with the grandparents, not to blah blah blah, you name it, he opposed it.

He defied and breached existing orders too. So, after consistent denial and defiance of almost everything that I requested, spoke of and anticipated, I had no other choice than to seek the court's assistance once again.

Fortunately, I was able to include all the previous documentation and evidence along with the current final order and present my submissions to the Judge. This time I'd travelled to Brisbane to get the first available court date, and was before a new Judge. I was still nervous and anxious, and my anxiety 'butterflies' were causing chaos in my stomach. No matter how many times I appeared in court, I was always nervous.

As my ex failed to turn up, the Judge heard what I had to say, recognised the challenges and amended the original final order to incorporate sole parental responsibility. This basically meant I was able to make decisions without the agreement of my ex. As previously mentioned in Chapter Three, sole parental responsibility is not given lightly, so this was a big win for me and the children. Now they could be enrolled in school, renew their passports and visit their grandparents and extended family in the UK.

Moving On

After three years of being involved in court proceedings, it was time to move on. I set some boundaries for my ex (which were ignored, predictably). I moved house, again. I also set up my separation support services business and was able to help others through their separation experience.

That was nearly a decade ago, and today I am happy to say that I continue to support those who are thinking of separating, those who have recently separated, those who are already involved in legal proceedings, and those who are post separation.

Having separated and been involved in legal proceedings myself, paired with my psychology background and my 30 years involvement in personal development, I feel I am well positioned to support others who are going through a similar experience. More importantly I am happy to do so, it gives me a sense of purpose and what better way to add value to others than to help them cope, be inspired and ultimately live their best life.

My life is very different to how it was when I first separated.

I've since moved on, in all ways. I am happy and healthy and the children are happy and healthy too. We have progressed through the ups and downs of my ex's departure, not only his initial exit but the subsequent trail of destruction in his wake; leaving us financially damaged and emotionally challenged.

Fortunately, the children are their very own success stories, and I am so proud of them. Not only are they doing exceptionally well in school they are also doing well within their social networks and relationships, their other activities including work commitments, and with driving lessons just around the corner it's a joy to see them embracing their independence and being confident to go out into the world. Both know exactly what they want to do in their career paths and though they are polar opposites, I've no doubt they'll make a positive impact in their chosen specialised areas.

I've spent over a decade dedicating my time to raising the children as a single parent 100% of the time. To this day there's still no physical, emotional or financial support from their father and there are no other family members around for support either.

Socialising has been limited, that said I've been able to grab a little balance between parenting 100% of the time and a meal out with girlfriends, or playdates and park picnics.

Once the children became teenagers, I was able to socialise again, alone, without them coming along. And with both of them encouraging me to find a 'boyfriend', dating was back on the agenda.

Marvellous Men and The Dating Scene

I wanted to meet someone organically and a few years ago I was very blessed to meet a special man who had a significantly positive impact on me and my children. He was caring, hardworking, confident, attentive and generous, and the perfect positive male role model. My ex left when the children were very young, so they have very little memory of him and the situation. When my male friend came along, the timing was perfect. It also helped that he was a tall, sexy, handsome man, and being able to laugh again, well, that was the cherry on the top for me.

Seeing the healthy interactions between me and my male friend, which included the children in a variety of activities from meals out, Mother's Day and Father's Day celebrations, to family events, day trips and sleepovers, meant my children were exposed to a kind of healthy man/woman 'normality'.

Plus, when my parents visited from the UK, we all spent quality time together, he won them over too! I'll be forever grateful for his arrival and presence in our lives. Even though he now has a long-term girlfriend we are still friends who get to reminisce occasionally about the 'old days', highlight stories of the present and share thoughts of the future.

I believe it's my time to put myself out there and explore the option of meeting someone who I can spend time with, be myself around and potentially spend my future with.

At the continuous badgering from friends, I spent a week embracing an online dating site. Let's explore that and dissect the results!

The forum I used was an app that gives the woman the control in initial communication. I now understand the concept of 'swipe right'!

A girlfriend and I spent over three hours one evening reviewing and swiping to compile a shortlist of potential suitors. What fun we had! The reality of the situation though, well, that's a different story; heard of breadcrumbing, benching and ghosting? Well, let me shed some light on that.

- Breadcrumbing: sending playful but noncommittal text messages, without exerting much effort.
- Benching: stringing someone along without committing.
- Ghosting: abruptly ceasing to contact someone, instead of telling them directly.

So, after identifying my top six (six is always my magic number) I contacted each of them individually, here's how it turned out:

Number 1: Mr E made me feel desirable! Plenty of fun banter, yet this ultimately became a breadcrumbing, benching situation. We never met.

Number 2: Mr T and I had some fun texting and arranged a proper meet-up at my local 'bar', met, laughed, 'proper' goodnight kiss, then…..nothing! He ghosted me! Onwards.

Number 3: Mr C seemed like a genuine guy, and I was impressed with his text conversation and work ethic, though after I left a voicemail (called him at his request) he 'disappeared'. Maybe it was my English accent or my throaty tones (I had a sore throat that day). Either way, another ghosting.

Number 4: Mr M and I met for coffee, nice enough guy but not for me.

Number 5: Mr N was a local guy, good conversationalist, great grammar (always a plus in my book, literally), arranged morning coffee – he didn't even show up! What the? I got 'benched' and 'ghosted' again!

Number 6: Mr L, a professional guy just looking for sex, which wasn't what I was after.

So that was my online dating experience. I was a busy bee but no one really wanted me for me. After my week online I signed off, deleted my account and haven't been back since.

I feel it's important to recognise and acknowledge the strong men that may already be in your life. I have three stand outs in mine. First is my Dad. I love him unconditionally; he is a strong, generous, loving man who has always had my back. He has always been there for me and his grandchildren, and he continues to be my rock.

Second, my friend and mentor Graham, who over the past 25+ years has been there through thick and thin, without physical distance or time difference getting in the way. He's guided me through business aspirations and decisions as well as the business of life!

The last is another 20+ year old friendship which continues to be an almost weekly dialogue and my 'go to' male perspective, discussing everything from music, to sex, drugs and rock'n'roll! The banter flows and I'm guaranteed a laugh every single time.

Before I move on from my online 'dates' and the marvellous men in my life, one man I haven't mention is our 'adopted' grandad, Mike. Mike is 90 years old and has been in my life for the past 13 years. I met him whilst hunting down some bargain clothes for the children at the local Vinnie's op shop. His wit, smile and generosity were a standout and we continued to stay friends when the op shop relocated. Over the years Mike has been another positive male role model in the children's lives. He ended up being my 'go to' handyman, always ready with his tools to repair anything that needed some attention. When my folks visited, I introduced them to Mike and Mike to them, the relationship blossomed and we are all firm friends to this day.

Way back when I first separated, my ex must have 'questioned' the children about my relationships. After spending the day with the children, my ex had made a huge assumption, as was highlighted in his subsequent email where he mentioned that my, 'new boyfriend Mike better know what he's in for'! Oh, how we laughed!

I am so grateful for the positive and supportive people in my life, both myself and the children are truly blessed to be surrounded by people who care about us. I have friends to laugh with and friends to confide in. I've friends to go out and have a good time with, and friends who'll just sit quietly with me as we pass the nibbles and pour wine together.

Helping Others

Today I spend my time coaching, mentoring, writing and speaking to individuals who want to live their best life, whether that's from the rubble of a relationship breakdown or from the muddled mindset of missed mojos!

I'm happy to say that what transpired all those years ago has presented me with many opportunities to help others. Though it certainly wasn't an overnight win.

There's no denying that the past ten plus years of being a single parent raising the children on my own has had its challenges, particularly after spending over three years involved in legal proceedings and 'wasting' what little money I had within the court process.

Though if that hadn't happened, neither would this book. I am grateful for each experience in my life and the opportunity to share some of those experiences with you along with techniques, perspectives and insights into how to make the best of a challenging situation.

Every experience, every person, every encounter, easy or challenging, is there to help guide you on your way to your purpose and living your best life. Embrace it. Enjoy it.

If you'd like to know more about what has been mentioned in this book, including my story, helpful tools and techniques, resources, website links and more, head on over to: www.helenslater.com.au.

HELPFUL WEBSITES AND RESOURCES

HELPLINES:

1800Respect –1800 737 732 Open 24 hours to support people impacted by sexual assault, domestic or family violence and abuse - https://www.1800respect.org.au/

Beyond Blue - 1300 224 636, webchat or email (24 hours/7 days) - https://www.beyondblue.org.au/

Lifeline - 13 11 14 (24 hours/7 days) or chat to a crisis supporter online (7pm – midnight/7 nights) - https://www.lifeline.org.au/

Seminars for separating individuals - http://separationinsights.com/

Government support services for separated parents - https://www.servicesaustralia.gov.au/individuals/separated-parents

Family Relationships - https://www.familyrelationships.gov.au/home

Relationships Australia - http://www.relationships.org.au/

Family Court of Australia - http://www.familycourt.gov.au/wps/wcm/connect/fcoaweb/home

Family Court of Australia – Court Fees (Family Law) - http://www.familycourt.gov.au/wps/wcm/connect/fcoaweb/forms-and-fees/fees-and-costs/fees

Federal Circuit Court of Australia - http://www.federalcircuitcourt.gov.au/wps/wcm/connect/fccweb/home

Federal Circuit Court of Australia – Court Fees (Family Law) - http://www.federalcircuitcourt.gov.au/wps/wcm/connect/fccweb/forms-and-fees/fees-and-costs/fees-fl/family-law-fees

The Commonwealth Courts Portal - https://www.comcourts.gov.au/

BIBLIOGRAPHY

Articles, Books, Reports

Albert Mehrabian, *Silent Messages* (Wadsworth Publishing Company, edition, 1971)

Domestic Violence Prevention Centre (DVPC), *The Purple Book*, (DVPC, 2020) 7

Eric Berne, *Games People Play: The Basic Handbook of Transactional Analysis*, (Ballantine Books, edition, 1996)

Joseph Luft 'The Johari Window: A Graphic Model of Awareness in Interpersonal Relations (1982) *Reading Book for Human Rights Training* <http://www.convivendo.net/wp-content/uploads/2009/05/johari-window-articolo-originale.pdf>

LexisNexis, *Concise Australian Legal Dictionary* (4th ed, 2011)

Ralph Waldo Emerson, *The Works of Ralph Waldo Emerson* (Fireside Edition Vol. 12)

Cases

Kowaliw & Kowaliw (1981) FLC 91-092

Legislation

Child Support (Assessment) Act 1989 *(Cth)* s 5

Family Law Act 1975 (Cth) (The Act) ss 79(4) and 75(2)

Family Law Rules 2004 (Cth) (The Rules)

Legal Profession Uniform Law Australian Solicitor's Conduct Rules 2015, reg. 10

Telecommunications and Postal Services Act 1989 Cth s 85L(b)

Other

Australian Association of Collaborative Professionals, 'What is collaborative practice' (Web Page, 24 October 2020) <https://www.collaborativeaustralia.com.au/>

Australian Government, 'Compare your child support collection options' (Web Page, 8 November 2020) <https://www.servicesaustralia.gov.au/individuals/services/child-support/child-support-assessment/how-manage-your-assessment/compare-your-child-support-collection-options>

DV Connect, 'Domestic Violence Statistics', (Web Page, 26 October 2020) <https://www.dvconnect.org/about/domestic-violence-statistics/>

Family Court of Australia, 'Children and Separation', (Web Page, 7 November 2020) <http://www.familycourt.gov.au>

Federal Circuit Court of Australia, 'Dispute Resolution in Family Law Proceedings', Federal Circuit Court of Australia (Web Page, 21 October 2020) <http://www.federalcircuitcourt.gov.au>

Gary Chapman, 'The 5 Love Languages', (Web Page, 21 October 2020) <www.5lovelanguages.com>

Geoff Brailey, 'Australia's Latest Marriage and Divorce Data', McCrindle (Web Page, 21 October 2020) <https://mccrindle.com.au/insights/blog/australias-latest-marriage-and-divorce-data/>

Performance Consultants, 'The Grow Model' (Web Page, 13 November 2020) <https://www.performanceconsultants.com/grow-model>

Redbook, *'About Us'*, (Webpage, 30 October 2020), <https://www.redbook.com.au/info/about-us>

NOTES

Chapter 1

1. Geoff Brailey, 'Australia's Latest Marriage and Divorce Data', McCrindle (Web Page, 21 October 2020) <https://mccrindle.com.au/insights/blog/australias-latest-marriage-and-divorce-data/>.
2. Federal Circuit Court of Australia, 'Dispute Resolution in Family Law Proceedings', Federal Circuit Court of Australia (Web Page, 21 October 2020) <http://www.federalcircuitcourt.gov.au/wps/wcm/connect/fccweb/family-law-matters/family-dispute-resolution>.
3. Gary Chapman, 'The 5 Love Languages', (Web Page, 21 October 2020) <www.5lovelanguages.com>.
4. DV Connect, 'Domestic Violence Statistics', (Web Page, 26 October 2020) <https://www.dvconnect.org/about/domestic-violence-statistics/>.
5. Domestic Violence Prevention Centre (DVPC), *The Purple Book*, (DVPC, 2020) 7.
6. Ibid.
7. DVPC (n8).
8. Ibid.
9. Ibid.
10. Ibid.
11. *Telecommunications and Postal Services Act 1989* (Cth) s 85L(b).
12. DVPC (n8).
13. Ibid.
14. Ibid.
15. Ibid.
16. In the interest of accuracy, the term peacock is commonly used to describe both the male and female of the species, however, technically only the males are peacocks, females are peahens and as a collective they are called peafowl. If in doubt, check with David Attenborough!

Chapter 2

1. *Family Law Act 1975* (Cth) (The Act) ss 79(4) and 75(2).
2. Ibid s 79 (4)(b).
3. Ibid ss 79(4) and 75(2).
4. Ibid s 4.
5. Ibid s 90(AD)(2).
6. *Family Law Rules* 2004 (Cth) (The Rules).
7. LexisNexis, *Concise Australian Legal Dictionary* (4th ed, 2011) 'disclosure' 178.
8. LexisNexis (n26) 'discovery' 179.
9. Redbook, '*About Us*', (Webpage, 30 October 2020), < https://www.redbook.com.au/info/about-us>.
10. The Act (n20) ss 79(4) and 75(2).
11. LexisNexis (n26) 'mortgage' 385.
12. The Act (n20) s 79(4)(b).
13. Ibid.
14. Ibid s 79(4)(c).
15. Ibid s 75(2).
16. Ibid s 75(2)(a).
17. Ibid s 75(2)(b).
18. Ibid s 75(2)(c).
19. Ibid s 75(2)(d).
20. Ibid s 75(2)(e).
21. Ibid s 75(2)(f).
22. Ibid s 75(2)(g).
23. Ibid s 75(2)(h).
24. Ibid s 75(2)(k).
25. Ibid s 75(2)(l).
26. Ibid s 75(2)(m).
27. Ibid s 75(2)(na).
28. Ibid s 75(2)(o).
29. Ibid s 75(2)(p).
30. *Kowaliw & Kowaliw* (1981) FLC 91-092.
31. Ibid.
32. The Rules (n25) rule 13.04.
33. The Act (n20) s 75(2).
34. *Kowaliw* (n49).

Chapter 3

1. The Act (n20) s 61DA.
2. Ibid.
3. Ibid s 61B.
4. Ibid s 60CC(2)(a).
5. Ibid s 60CC(2)(b).
6. Ibid s 61DA(3)(a).
7. Ibid s 61DA(3)(b).
8. Ibid s 61DA(3)(d).
9. Ibid s 61DA(3)(c).
10. Ibid s 61DA(3)(e).
11. Ibid.
12. Ibid s 61DA(3)(f).
13. Ibid s 61DA(3)(h).
14. Ibid s 61DA(3)(j).
15. Ibid s 61DA(3)(m).
16. Ibid s 63C(1).
17. LexisNexis (n26) 'consent order' 118.
18. Ibid s 64B(1).
19. The Act (n20) s 112AD.
20. The Act (n20).
21. Ibid.
22. Family Court of Australia, 'Children and Separation', (Web Page, 7 November 2020) <http://www.familycourt.gov.au/wps/wcm/connect/fcoaweb/family-law-matters/parenting/children-and-separation/children-and-separation>.
23. Eric Berne, *Games People Play: The Basic Handbook of Transactional Analysis*, (Ballantine Books, edition, 1996)
24. 1975.
25. Ibid.
26. Ibid s 68M(2).
27. Ibid.
28. Ibid.
29. *Child Support (Assessment) Act* 1989 *(Cth)* s 5.
30. The Act (n20) s 66K.
31. Australian Government, 'Compare your child support collection options' (Web Page, 8 November 2020) <https://www.servicesaustralia.gov.au/indi-

viduals/services/child-support/child-support-assessment/how-manage-your-assessment/compare-your-child-support-collection-options>.

Chapter 4

1. Family Court of Australia (n76) 'Property and finances after separation'.
2. Federal Circuit Court, (n4) 'How do I apply for a Divorce?'.
3. Ibid.
4. Family Court of Australia (n76).
5. Ibid.
6. Ibid.
7. Ibid.
8. Ibid.
9. LexisNexis (n26).
10. Federal Circuit Court (n4).
11. Ibid.
12. The Act (n20) s 60I.
13. Ibid.
14. Ibid.
15. Ibid.
16. The Rules (n25) rule 13.05.
17. Ibid.
18. LexisNexis (n26) 'affidavit' 20.
19. Family Court of Australia (n76) 'Preparing an affidavit'.
20. Ibid.
21. Federal Circuit Court of Australia (n4) 'Notice of child abuse, family violence or risk'.
22. Family Court of Australia (n76) 'How do I serve court documents?'.
23. The Rules (n25) rule 7.04.
24. Ibid rule 7.12.
25. Federal Circuit Court of Australia (n4) 'Response'.
26. The Rules (n25) subrule 4.03(2).
27. Family Court of Australia (n76) 'Response to initiating application'.
28. The Rules (n25) subrule 4.08(1).
29. The Act (n20) s 112AD.
30. Ibid.
31. Federal Circuit Court of Australia (n4) 'Application – Contravention'.
32. LexisNexis (n26) 'Statute of Limitation'.

33. Family Court of Australia (n76) 'Property and finances after separation'.
34. LexisNexis (n26) 'De facto relationship'.
35. Albert Mehrabian, *Silent Messages* (Wadsworth Publishing Company, edition, 1971).
36. Ralph Waldo Emerson, *The Works of Ralph Waldo Emerson* (Fireside Edition Vol. 12).
37. LexisNexis (n26) 'interim' 313.
38. Performance Consultants, 'The Grow Model' (Web Page, 13 November 2020) <https://www.performanceconsultants.com/grow-model>.

Chapter 5

1. Australian Association of Collaborative Professionals, https://www.collaborativeaustralia.com.au/
2. *Legal Profession Uniform Law Australian Solicitor's Conduct Rules* 2015, reg. 10.
3. Joseph Luft 'The Johari Window: A Graphic Model of Awareness in Interpersonal Relations (1982) *Reading Book for Human Rights Training* <http://www.convivendo.net/wp-content/uploads/2009/05/johari-window-articolo-originale.pdf>.
4. Federal Circuit Court of Australia (n4).
5. (Qld) 2007.

ABOUT THE AUTHOR

Helen is a 'Mindset Mentor' who helps people embrace change, particularly those who are going through life challenges.

Originally from the UK, Helen came to Australia in 2002 where she fell in love with the Sunshine Coast and has been based there ever since.

Single mum to two teenagers, she's had her fair share of life challenges, from work and relationship challenges, relocation and financial challenges, to being embroiled in the Australian Family Law legal system and subsequently self-representing.

Working with her clients, she helps them to embrace change by empowering them with a positive mindset, through focus, knowledge and action, all the while providing empathy, so that they can realise their goals and live their best life!

Helen is a mentor to a variety of individuals: from busy mums to business owners, tenacious teens and energetic entrepreneurs, separating couples, divorcees and families as well as those seeking independence in life. She's also a blue card holder, a trained foster carer, and has helped teenagers and tweens through their own life challenges.

As well as academic achievements in psychology and coaching, she has over thirty years' experience in personal development, from training to consulting, coaching to mentoring. Helen believes in life balance and alignment and is a certified remedial massage therapist. An avid reader, a keen writer, lover of music and self-confessed coffee lover.

All that said, her vision is to help as many people as possible to embrace change and live their best life with a sense of purpose and fun. Make money, be inspired and have fun in the process. It really is as simple and as complicated as that!

Start small go big!

www.helenslater.com.au

www.ingramcontent.com/pod-product-compliance
Lightning Source LLC
Chambersburg PA
CBHW021405290426
44108CB00010B/387